The Lord's Prayer
and the
Inner Life

T. Craig Isaacs

The Lord's Prayer and the Inner Life
Copyright © 2025
T. Craig Isaacs, Ph.D.

Library of Congress
Control Number:

ISBN: ISBN: 978-0-9886645-2-4

FOR MORE INFORMATION CONTACT:
T. Craig Isaacs, Ph.D.
drcraigisaacs@aol.com
drcraigisaacs.com

Contents

New Wine   7

Intimacy   27

The Fullness of Life   33

Provision for the Journey   41

Forgiveness   55

Temptation and Evil   67

The Essence of Jesus' Prayer   85

New Wine

Deciding to read this book likely indicates you are interested in developing your spiritual life, if even only to a small degree. Most likely you are a person looking for further guidance in the life of prayer; searching for even greater clarity regarding how to live a truly spiritual life. Assuming this is true, I hope that you will walk with me on this journey. My prayer is that you find what you encounter here to be at minimum a boost toward living the life that has secretly resided in your soul. May you find this a springboard from which to launch out on the wondrous adventure of watchfulness and prayer; to endeavor to place a foot across the threshold of the thin place between this overt world of the senses and the inner—often seemingly elusive—world of the Kingdom of God.

To begin we need to discuss such thoughts as, "How do I live a spiritual life in the midst of such a demanding world?" "How am I to pray?" "What does it mean to be spiritual?" Even "What actually is prayer?" The answers to these questions have filled copious volumes, lectures, sermons, and discussions, as they will continue to do.

Why so many books? Why are so many answers necessary? The mere number of books makes it obvious that, in some manner or another, the answers presented must not have been fully satisfying to their readers. If they were satisfactory, then only a few truly good books would suffice to fill the void. This is not to imply that these books and teachings are in some way wrong. Even though a great number of these explanations may be lacking in depth, it is probably not the authors' fault which leads to this proliferation, to the constant demand for another answer. There may be a more troubling reason. The cause may be more an unrecognized resistance, a subtle realization that if we truly grasp the meaning of prayer, it will compel us toward a complete and astonishing transformation of our life. Many of us are reticent to embrace such a dramatic transformation. Isaiah said as much, and Jesus quotes him, saying "hearing they do not hear, and seeing they do not see, they do not want to hear and see, because if they did then they would have to turn and seek God."[1]

Still, many seekers want to better their spiritual lives. We want the benefits of prayer and meditation. The trouble is that too often we desire these benefits on our own terms. We want the spiritual to be a part of our life, possibly even a generous slice. But this is the problem: prayer cannot be a mere part of our life. To understand prayer and the spiritual life is to appreciate that it is not a portion but rather the fullness of life itself. We will never understand how to pray as long as prayer is seen as a technique that merely affirms one aspect of our lives. We will never understand the spiritual life as long as it is perceived as only a segment in the full cafeteria line of our existence. We like to think that our spiritual life can exist alongside our secular life; that we have a time of being spiritual, and a time for doing business; a time for family, and a time for recreation. Our list goes on. We err when we conceive of prayer as one activity among many, a spiritual technique that we perform at a certain time of the day and week. Jesus shatters this idea when he declares:

> If anyone comes to me and does not hate his own father and mother and wife and children and brothers and sisters, yes, and even his own life, he cannot be my disciple.[2]

As long as we see prayer as an isolated activity, and the spiritual life as simply one aspect of my whole being, we will continue to futilely search through thousands of books and lectures, never finding the answer to what prayer is. Because the true answer is more demanding than we may want, and so we search for easier solutions.

---

[1] Matthew 13:3
[2] Luke 14:26

The answer is also illusive because we have been looking at the question of prayer while facing in the wrong direction. To reach for an answer to the question of prayer we need to change our perspective, to alter our paradigm. We need a change of mind, or as Jesus proclaims, we need to repent. We need a metanoia.

The word *metanoia* is a powerful word throughout the New Testament. Frequently it is translated as repent. However, this word now typically carries the conception of ending one's sinful behaviors. Though this reading has some limited merit it misses the deeper point. The deeper point implies the taking on of a completely new way of thinking which only then has the consequence of a new, virtuous manner of behaving.

Metanoia is a derivation of two Greek words, *meta*—beyond or after—and *gnosis*—to think or know. It implies a change to our way of knowing, a looking beyond our own conceptions and assumptions, and the gaining of a possibly startling new perspective. What is this new and more expansive perspective? It is seeing prayer and the complete spiritual life as one and the same, prayer is not an isolated act. For the sake of emphasis we say once again, prayer is not *an aspect* of one's spiritual life but *is* the spiritual life.

Prayer is commonly understood as something we *do*; our new perspective is to see prayer as something we *are*. To live a spiritual life is to be a prayer. This is what Jesus taught his disciples when they came to the point of that momentous request: "Lord, teach us to pray." Let us pause and recall that incident described to us in the Gospel of Luke[3].

We do not know what type of day it was, maybe it was just a typical day in the village of Bethany. Jesus and his disciples had earlier been invited to dine in the house of Martha and Mary. It was a time of sundry emotions, a moment of varied sentiments. There was a sense of awe in the air, a sense of something important

---

[3] Luke 10:38ff

happening, something that one could not quite put a finger on, yet portentous all the same.

There was also an ambience of anxiety. A pull to fall into the atmosphere of the holy that was surrounding them while at the same time the desire to maintain decorum as Martha attempts to prepare a proper meal for her guests. In this mix of awe and anxiety we find Jesus calmly talking and teaching. We all know the story, how Martha—in her desire to meet the material needs of her guests—grows angry with her sister Mary for bathing herself in the atmosphere of awe. How Jesus gently reprimands Martha by telling her that Mary has chosen the good portion in life, hanging upon Jesus' every word and divine presence.

We are not told how the scene ends, but later we find Jesus outside, revitalizing his own inner life. We can almost see him, kneeling on the rough earth, his eyes closed, his inner eyes opened to heaven, a calmness surrounding his very being, a calmness enveloping the environment about him. Even the disciples, who also endured the earlier tension of the home, must have felt the restoring calm as they watched him, for out of this moment one of them had the courage and eagerness to ask the vital question: "Lord, teach *us* to pray..." Jesus, arising may have looked at him with a riveting and loving gaze and then began:

> When you pray, you must not be like the hypocrites; for they love to stand and pray in the synagogues and at the street corners, that they may be seen by men. Truly I say to you, they have received their reward.[4]

A familiar image would have immediately risen in their minds. They would have recalled the many times that they had seen the important men of the synagogue and villages, dressed in their best garb, hands raised to heaven, calling upon God in most pious tones, appearing very devout and important to many, but continuing to experience in their own souls a sense of inner

---

[4] Matthew 6:5

emptiness; an emptiness revealing the meaninglessness and futility they secretly felt during their times of prayer. An emptiness that engenders a doubt that prayer even works. But if that is not the way to pray, then how? Gratefully, Jesus continued and answered this lingering question.

> And when you pray, go into your room and shut the door and pray to your Father who is in secret; and your Father who sees in secret will reward you.[5]

"Very good," they might have said, "I will not pray in a manner for others to admire me, or where others may think me spiritual or pious, I will do it only for God's approval." They might have thought, "Good, now I've got the right attitude, but what then am I to say? What am I to do? What is it that you were just doing, Master? Is there a special phrase to utter, a secret word to say? Is there a special image, a secret thought to ponder when I pray?" Jesus anticipated these questions and responded:

> And in praying do not heap up empty phrases as the Gentiles do; for they think that they will be heard for their many words. Do not be like them, for your Father knows what you need before you ask him.[6]

With this each of them could certainly recollect various scenes to which Jesus was alluding. They might have recalled certain foreigners speaking of going to the ceremonies where alcohol and other intoxicants were imbibed, bringing upon themselves an ecstasy through which they hoped the gods would communicate. They might recall the stories from the Scriptures, where Elijah would confront the priests of Baal dancing and cutting themselves as they shouted to the skies for their god to act. In his mind's eye, another could see a man sitting in the street, cross-legged, meditating upon some indiscernible image. Still another might wonder about friends he knew that had entered the secret

---

[5] Matthew 6:6
[6] Matthew 6:7

societies in the hills where they would learn the special ways to meditate, secret knowledge that they were told would lead to enlightenment. Formerly, all these thoughts may have sparked an interest—maybe a little envy—in our hearers, for these gentiles seemed to know more about the spiritual life than they did. However, Jesus now says to them, do not follow their example.

He tells them this because all these methods attest to the false principle that prayer is a special part, and therefore only a segment, of one's full life. Jesus wishes to take his disciples in a totally different direction. He exclaims that prayer is not a technique, not a program or method. It is not a means to ecstasy. It is not a way of getting in touch with or moving God to act only when you need Him. It is not a way of gaining a special gift, or an arcane knowledge of a superior world. This may have been how others had seen it, but if it is seen as such, we will need a plethora of teachings and books. Jesus disavows the concept that prayer is a technique in favor of a new thinking: prayer *is* the spiritual life.

Due to our exaggerated materialistic and positivistic outlook on existence, prayer is today conceived as merely a technique even more than it may have been in ancient times. The modern person has come to view reality through the lens of modernism and post-modernism, philosophies which lend themselves to a mechanistic and materialistic view of reality. In such a view prayer can only be a technique.

Peter Krefft[7] has outlined three philosophies that have guided much of our thinking over the past two thousand years; these are traditionalism (or pre-modernism), modernism (or rationalism), and postmodernism (or what he calls irrationalism). In more descriptive language he calls these the philosophies of moreness, sameness, and lessness. In relation to our understanding of the life, moreness could also be called mysticism; that is, there is more to the world than is seen, or as he quotes Shakespeare "There

---

[7] Krefft,Peter (2018). *Doors in the Walls of the World*. Ignatius Press, San Franciso.

are more things in heaven and earth, Horatio, than are dreamt of in your philosophy."

Sameness is a rationalism (modernism) that conceives that all things are identical, or the same, to what we think they are. "[A]s Hegel put it, 'that which is real is rational and that which is rational is real.' In other words, he says, we are know-it-alls: what is inside our mind and what is outside match pretty perfectly. To believe that, you have to be either a genius, or very arrogant, or both (like Hegel)." This was where much of the 20th Century was stuck.

Then there is the philosophy of lessness, of reductionism, which dominates much thinking at this moment. You can observe it in medicine and psychology where all behaviors and experiences are presently reduced to neurological functioning and brain structures. Obviously, these three philosophies diverge on how one understands the universe surrounding them.

To understand Jesus demands that we return to the philosophy of moreness. He showed us that reality is encountered first and foremost in what we call the inner world of the soul. That even the Church has forgotten this is well illustrated in the modern tendency to translate Jesus' acclamation "The Kingdom of God is within you," as "The Kingdom of God is amongst you."[8] The Greek word in question is rightly translated in either manner, yet in our materialistic age, our bias is toward the outer world and so the community focused word of "amongst" whereas in the apostolic age and time of the early Church Fathers it was understood in the manner closer to Jesus' teaching, as an inner reality.

Without embracing the fact that there is a deeper inner life and significance of that inner life, we over-value the "reality" of the outer life, becoming principally outer-directed. Such an orientation offers only opportunities for literalism and concretization.

---

[8] Luke 17:21

Positivistic and humanistic rationalists bewail the fact that religious fundamentalists take the scriptures too literally. However, the problem is not a conflict of literal understanding versus allegorical or cultural, but rather a problem of inner versus outer. On this, the religious fundamentalist and the scientific positivist unwittingly agree. The foundation of both of their arguments is an outer, materialistic orientation by which they approach the spiritual life. Both are making the materialistic error of seeing outer reality as the only "true" reality neglecting the inner reality of the spirit and the psyche. Jesus takes us in a different direction. It is by regarding that the kingdom is within the depths of your soul that you can genuinely approach an understanding of how to live this inner life of prayer.

What then is this psyche, this soul? We begin by conceiving of the individual as comprised of a vast inner world of which the psyche—or soul—is but one aspect, and that within the psyche is a function we recognize as the ego which is an even smaller part of our inner life. We understand this as we receive the answer given in a broad stroke as we read the first chapters of Genesis. There we are told that the human being—and therefore the human psyche—is formed in the image of God. This implies that the human being corresponds in a reflective manner to the Holy Trinity.

Just as the Holy Trinity is comprised of three persons who are in essence the same, so too the intrapsychic nature of the human being is comprised of three parts all of the same essence. What this means specifically with the Holy Trinity has been the subject of numerous able descriptions, but for our purpose we will confine ourselves to the explanation of the Holy Trinity closely allied with traditional Augustinian thought and that of St. Thomas Aquinas. Paraphrasing their thought, we may understand the conception of the Holy Trinity in the following manner.

The Father—who is beyond all form and conception—begets the Son, an image of Himself but one that can have form and also brings forth all form as the Word. At this point we regard

God Who is beyond form begetting God who has form. Then, when the Father sees the Son he breathes forth loving union toward his image. When the begotten Son looks back and sees the Father—from whom he emerged—he likewise breathes forth love toward the Father. Archbishop Fulton Sheen is known to have poetically described this breathing forth as a sigh of loving ecstasy. This is the Holy Breath, the Holy Sigh, the Holy Spirit; the third person of the Trinity.

This sigh, this breathing forth of love, is eternally immediate. Not two breaths but one occurring in an eternal moment. The Second Council of Lyon stated it most clearly: "the Holy Spirit proceeds eternally from the Father and the Son, not as from two principles, but from one, not by two aspirations, but by one only." This third person of the Trinity, the Holy Spirit, binds the Father and the Son together eternally in love and so the three are an eternal unity. Here is a simple and beautiful description of the Holy Trinity.

Let us relate this description to the human inner life. When conceived in the womb, the person is in a place of formlessness much as we understand would be analogous with the Heavenly Father. In much of the literature on Biblical anthropology this has been referred to as the human spirit. I choose to call it the deep-self, merely because the term spirit carries so many meanings that its use often becomes more clouded and confusing than helpful.

After the conception of the deep-self sometime later there emerges from it an image of that deep-self, a form that we recognize as the psyche or soul. As with the term spirit, soul carries so much baggage that I have found it useful to utilize its Greek translation, psyche. Traditionally we then have the soul emerging from the spirit but being the form-giving image of that spirit, the abode of thoughts and feelings. It is within the psyche that still another part forms, a part we call the ego. When functioning ideally, the ego which is the center of consciousness, of will, and of intellect works to bring balance and wholeness to the fullness of the psyche.

Ideally, the emergent psyche develops over time to become the perfect image of its originator, the deep-self. As it was with the Holy Trinity, so it is with the inner life. The deep-self is to look upon the psyche as the Father looked upon the Son and bind to it in love. The psyche—by means of the conscious functioning of the ego—looks back at the deep-self as the Son did to the Father and it also breaths forth a humble, self-giving love toward its originating image, the deep-self.

Here is where we run into a significant difference between the eternally perfect Holy Trinity and its image reflected in the human being. At the moment of begetting within the Trinity there is an instantaneous and singular aspiration of the spirit of love between the two; the singular procession of the Holy Spirit from the Father and the Son. In God, the eternal now of the originator and the image is immediate, the image does not develop over time but merely is. In the human inner life this does not appear to be the case. The psyche, the begotten image, appears to develop over time. During that development the psyche by means of the ego is learning about itself and learning to turn toward the deep-self with a selfless bond of love. With the Holy Trinity this is an eternal fact, with the human image it is a process; one that can go awry and needs assistance.

So, we conceive of the healthy inner life as an image of the Holy Trinity, with the deep-self and psyche in union with each other within a field of loving embrace, the ego working from within the psyche to bring this about.

This is what we understand Jesus meant by calling us to wholeness, maturity, and completeness, beckoning us to become whole and complete—perfect--even and the Father in Heaven is so perfect. We are to be at loving harmony within ourselves, our psyche in loving and humble connection to our deep-self and then that loving inner union of psyche to deep-self giving itself in loving harmony with the God.

This leads us to understand two important aspects of healthy psychic functioning. First is our recognition that the healthy psyche is called to be a reflected image of the deep-self. Second is that both the deep-self and the psyche are comprised of innumerable aspects or parts, with our present conscious identity (the ego) being merely one part.

Just as God is not a monistic oneness but a unity in Trinity or diversity, so too the deep-self and the psyche are not monistic unities but comprised of various aspects. Wholeness and health are then related to the harmonious functioning and interrelating of these parts. We see that a major responsibility of the ego is the coordination and harmonization of these diverse parts within the psyche.

To clarify, we speak of the begotten image in its complete, healthy nature as the psyche. The ego is the part of the psyche we recognize and refer to as "me" or "I". Now comes the problem. This ego tends to see itself not as a part but as the fullness of oneself. The other parts are either ignored completely or seen as subordinate to the ego. This is a problem. Humility and truth should ideally reveal to this ego that it is merely one part of the greater "I", the psyche, the begotten image of a deeper self. The totality that we call the person is a composite nature. The whole person is comprised of the deep self or spirit; the physical body; and psyche or soul. *Pneuma*, *Physis* and *Psyche*, comprise one human being who—when healthy—expresses and experiences these diverse parts in harmonious unison as beautiful choir of voices.

Already we begin to see that we are so much grander than the limited conception we presently have of ourselves. To shift our paradigm of thinking to embrace this trinitarian conception of the person is difficult but useful in then grasping the life of prayer.

Another manner of illustrating the inner dynamic is to see it picturesquely. Imagine it this way: your whole inner life as an ocean. Then think of your ego as one fish in this ocean. This fish experiences emotions and instincts. It also has a mind. Imagine that the rational mind is merely like the brain of that fish. The brain is very important but certainly not the complete fish, and the fish is certainly not as grand as the ocean. It is not even the only fish in the ocean. However, the fish likes to conceive of the ocean as "its" ocean (my inner life). The fish tends to believe that the waters around it are all relative to it, possibly even created by it.

Humility demands otherwise. The virtue of humility assists the fish to realize that the ocean is not a part of it, but that it is a part of the ocean. When this happens, the fish (recall this is the ego) takes the inner life (the life of the remainder of the psyche) seriously, even as the most enduring and real aspect of life. Humility brings the psychic system into order. This image of the fish and the ocean will aid us in our further understanding of a life of prayer.

With this picture we can lay hold of a simpler understanding of our lives. The ocean is our psyche, it is a reflection of the image of the deeper self which is a reflection of the God who created us. It is this deep-self which knew and intimately encountered God at the beginning. The psyche and its ego was always to be a part of this system, a reflection of the deep-self, but only a reflection. It should never have considered itself the whole.

To summarize: when we think of ourselves as an "I", a "this is me", we are identifying only with the fish, the ego which is only a part of the psyche which in turn is only one aspect of the full inner life of the self. In the beginning and in the end our identity is to be with both the ocean (the psyche) and the fish (the ego) as they relate to the deep-self. Like the Trinity, by means of the ego, the psyche and the deep-self should unite in love, where the psyche

18

recognizes that it is a reflected image of the deep-self and the deep-self is a reflection of God.

Unfortunately, this is not where things typically stand in any life and so the need for grace and salvation. Instead of a psyche that is in harmony within itself, the parts of the intended whole of the begotten reflection are broken apart. We know this as the Fall and the "fallen nature". Ideally, our psyche was to be a compendium of many parts just as our physical body is a compendium of many limbs and organs comprising a whole. The psyche no longer recognizes this and is dominated by the ego which was intended only to be a governing aspect of the psyche, not its identity. A dramatic aspect of the "fall" is the breaking apart of the psyche's sense of wholeness. The psyche's ego, rather than recognizing the wholeness of the inner life now identifies primarily with the physical body. It would be as if the physical body only recognized the head as its true self and the other limbs and organs as extraneous. The oddity of that thought is an illustration of the oddity of our present psychic existence.

Because of disorder within the psyche, the ego experiences that there are a multitude of other fish in the psychic ocean. These are felt as the other "voices" we hear in our head, the conflicting parts of the fullness of ourselves. Even though the ego has usurped its position and function within the economy of the inner life, still it is an important "fish" in this function of the psychic ocean. Its original function was to be the center of consciousness, and that role is still necessary for health and sanctification. The ego was, and is, to be like a flashlight in a dark room.

If we look at all of this in another way, we can imagine that, for a number of reasons, all tied to the theology of the Fall, our ocean has become rather dark and obscure. The ego experiences the remainder of the inner life as something odd and foreign. It disbelieves in the inner existence or at best calls it the unconscious. It minimizes its importance, forgetting dreams or seeing them as irrelevant. The ego acts like Ebenezar Scrooge when confronted with the ghost of Jacob Marley in "A Christmas Carol" when he defiantly rejects the reality of the spirit before saying: "You may be an undigested bit of beef, a blot of mustard, a crumb of cheese, a fragment of underdone potato. There's more of gravy than of grave about you, whatever you are!"

What we can see from our new spiritual perspective is that our problem has been that the desired deep-self to psyche relationship—this image of Trinity—that was intended to be fully conscious and a light became darkness, leaving only a speck of light shining. That speck is now the ego. And that speck of light, unaware of the vastness of the life of the soul around it, has taken the flashlight of awareness and turned it not to illuminate the inner darkness but to shine only on itself and the body. It is like a person in a dark room who has forgotten to explore the room but only turns the light on his own face, and becomes satisfied that illuminating himself is good enough. Is it any wonder that so many of us are neurotic and narcissistic?

Jesus, in his call to a transformed life, asks the ego to return to its created role; to turn the light outward into the soul, into the remainder of the psyche and toward the deep-self. It may be why throughout the Gospels Jesus is constantly calling his hearers to wake up, to stay alert, to be aware: to become conscious.

Now a final illustration. Recognizing that the psyche is populated with various parts, how are these parts to function together? One manner of thinking about this is to view this population as if it were a gigantic committee, where the ego is intended to chair the committee. The ego is to shine its light of consciousness on the various members, getting to know and understand the various desires and thoughts of each of them and then bringing these to the whole. In this act of consciousness of the parts now centered in the ego, the whole may come into a consensus. It is what Jesus may have been getting at when He calls us to be "perfect" even as the Father in heaven is perfect or, as the word is better translated today, to be in complete harmony, for the word perfect used in the New Testament is, in many ways, the equivalent of the Hebrew word shalom. Shalom is the peace of harmony. The ego's role is to be the chair of the committee, or the conductor of a choir, not attempting to produce a monotonous monotone, but a harmonious resonance of inner voices.

Now we may see that a task of the inner life is for the ego to take its flashlight of consciousness and shine it into the ocean of the soul. As it does this the inner life is painted with the light of consciousness until the soul is illuminated with light. Then the consensus arising from this light is submitted to God. The fullness of the psyche and deep-self unite with God and the words of the Psalmist echo back to us: "Bless the Lord, O my soul, and all that is within me, bless His Holy Name."[9] As we are about to see, this is the foundation of being a prayer.

God never stopped relating intimately to the full of ourselves. God speaks continuously to the deep-self and depths of the psyche, his voice and presence resound throughout the "ocean" of our inner lives. As the Psalmist said "deep calls unto deep"[10]. But even today, the ego demands that God speak to it rather than the ego seeking the voice and presence of God in the depths. Hearing God in the depths is His intended pattern. So a direct ego to God experience is a very rare encounter, one that usually only occurs when God is trying valiantly to get our attention. Once our attention is attained, He returns to the pattern he first intended.

If we are going to truly be in communion with God, if we are truly going to be a prayer and to pray, we need to adopt this new perspective, this new wine. God, knowing that this true change in perspective, the true *metanoia* is beyond our grasp, assists with His own energy, an energy we call grace. The ego merely needs to accept that this is true (to believe) and still itself (be still and know that I am God[11]) and look within with the attitude that it is only a

---

[9] Psalm 103:1
[10] Psalm 42:7
[11] Psalm 46:10

small part of that grand whole that God created as us. This is the ego's attitude of humility. When it does this, the beginning of full healing has begun (salvation). This is the simplicity of Jesus' teaching. What does it take to be healed, to be saved? To believe him.

As we consider the Christian approach to life, we must also take into account another important distinction that effects our understanding. Jesus has initiated a new way into the world, the way of the individuated person in an intimate relationship with God, of one who fully knows him or herself and submits this self to God. He has inaugurated a time of New Wine and so brought about the need for a new wineskin. We are to abandon the old wineskin of the former ways of seeking God, the old ways of religious life.

Throughout human history there have been two dominant approaches to the religious life. One—characteristic of hunting and gathering societies—was the way of the shaman. The shaman is often referred to as the medicine man or woman, or the witch-doctor. These were the highly respected, bearers of the group's wisdom. They knew how to traverse the spirit world. Because they would perform their duties and enter the spiritual realm on their own, the shaman appears on a superficial level to express an individually-oriented religious experience. However, as we look more closely, the shaman's self-awareness is still inexorably tied to the group identity as a whole. The shaman's identity is confined to his role as a part of the tribal group performing an integral function for the group. This is of interest to us because in many ways the path opened by Jesus would appear to be the old path of the shaman. We would need no new wineskin if the path of the shaman is what Jesus was proposing. However, as we will see, a new wineskin is necessary for the way of Jesus, a way that looks into the individual heart while still incorporating, yet transcending, the group.

The other way—characteristic of agriculturally-based societies—was the way of the priesthood. By the time of Jesus this was the most dominant form of religion in the Near East. The priest was the bearer of the culture's traditions and morals. The priest was the one who was designated by the community to approach God and intercede with God for the group. As with the shaman, the priesthood was not a pursuit of God by an individual for the individual, but a relationship determined by the roles and needs of the community. If the typical person wished to communicate with God, the standard was to do so through the priesthood and the confines of the rituals of the group. This is the old wine, the wine of community identity.

To hold this community identity one needed structures, and so arose the old wineskin of laws. This is clearly seen in Judaism, though it is evident in any agricultural or city-based society. To be related to God one needed either to be born a Jew or be adopted into the religion as a Jew. Once a Jew, the relationship with God was determined by the Law and the Prophets. The old wine of community identity and the old wineskin of the Law.

Jesus brought a new way, a new wine. This was the way of the individual relationship to God without outside mediation. This way became known as the Church, the priesthood of all believers. Not that all would take up the clerical identity or ritual role in society, but rather each was a priest in the sense that each was in personal, direct contact with God through the Spirit. Each believer was now a container and representative of the Law of God. No longer an outer law of community but an inner law of the Spirit.

This is profoundly illustrated for us on the day of Pentecost and the first baptism of the Holy Spirit. The Law of God was given corporately through Moses as wind and fire surrounded and descended upon Mount Sinai. The Law of the Spirit was given as wind and fire surrounded and descended individually upon each of the apostles and Mary.

This new wine would demand a new wineskin, for the old wineskin of the Law could not allow for, much less conceive of, an individual path. External laws by nature are for the functioning of the group, not for the operation of the individual inner life. So a new wineskin would be introduced; the wineskin of the law of the inner life, the Law of the Spirit.

Such a move was sure to create tension, for the disciple was now to follow a new way, without the clarity of the old boundaries, and old securities of the overt, outer Law. Even though that old law was fully alive within the Law of the Spirit (Jesus did not do away with the Law or the Prophets, but fulfilled them), still the Law of the Spirit would lead to interpretations that the outer law had not comprehended. Now one might be healing on the Sabbath and fulfilling the intent of the original law but would be in conflict with the community understanding. The disciple now was called upon to seek God person-to-person, heart-to-heart, and this could be both exciting, and disconcerting. John Sanford, in his book *The Kingdom Within*, has said it well:

> By instinct man is a group animal. For hundreds of thousands of years he has existed through the group, and the individual has found his identity and meaning by virtue of his inclusion in tribe, clan, nation. But the Kingdom of God calls us to go beyond this ancient herd instinct and to establish an individual consciousness of oneself and of God. Being a disciple means following the call to the individual Way, and inevitably this will mean the separating out of oneself from the collective psychology of the group. This tendency to submerge ourselves in the group is a principal source of our remaining unconscious and may exist with our Church, our family, our nation, our business, a branch of the armed services, whatever it is with which we define ourselves. Separating ourselves from the group identification is a painful process, for as long as we remain submerged in the group, we find a certain security. When this unconscious identification gives way, as it must under the impact of the kingdom of God, the illusory peace is shattered. So Jesus declares, 'Do not suppose that I have

come to bring peace to the earth: it is not peace I have come to bring, but a sword".[12]

To live in the manner of the new wine—to develop within the new wineskin of the Spirit—is painful, lonely, and often fearful. But it is the manner by which Jesus opens the way to God and the fullness of the spiritual life. If we do not accept this, then both experiencing and understanding Jesus' teaching on prayer and the spiritual life will be inhibited. It is one of the reasons that many do not find satisfaction in their spiritual lives. They are still attempting to interpret Jesus' teaching and leading by placing it in the realm of the old wineskin. So, we end up with versions of Christianity which look more like Judaism, merely with new wording for old laws, and a new vocabulary for the old demand to be a good member of the herd.

Jesus calls us out of the herd to develop ourselves. There will be a call to re-enter the community but initially, in order to develop one's personal life with God, the herd must be rejected. The old wineskin is to be left for what it was made for, and the new wineskin of Life in the Spirit embraced to live out the new wine of a full, individual life given to God.

This was prophetically pre-figured in the Old Testament wisdom book of the *Song of Songs*, a book that speaks to the binding love of the individual and God. There, in the first chapter, we read:

O that you would kiss me with the kisses of your mouth!
For your love is better than wine,
your anointing oils are fragrant,
your name is oil poured out;
therefore the maidens love you.
Draw me after you, let us make haste.
The king has brought me into his chambers.
We will exult and rejoice in you;
we will extol your love more than wine;

---

[12] Sanford, John (1970). <u>The Kingdom Within</u>. Lippincott, New York. p. 8

rightly do they love you.
I am very dark, but comely,
O daughters of Jerusalem,
like the tents of Kedar, like the curtains of Solomon.
Do not gaze at me because I am swarthy,
because the sun has scorched me.
My mother's sons were angry with me,
they made me keeper of the vineyards;
but, my own vineyard I have not kept! (v. 2-6)

"But my own vineyard I have not kept", cries the heart of the disciple. Jesus came and inaugurated the path of the individual. He has taken away the darkness that kept the person from God; he has heard the cries of those who worked only for the group, the herd, taking them from the scorching pain and anger of that duty, into the beauty of developing one's own spiritual life, one's own vineyard, to know the fullness of the love of God in each one's heart. This is the beginning of our understanding of the spiritual path of the new wine. Even though the community will, in the end, once again become important, it must first be rejected if we are to now know the way of Jesus' spiritual life for us, and for us to know how to pray.

How, then, do we pray? We walk the path of the inner life. How this is to be done is Jesus' answer to his disciples' question, an answer which begins: "Our Father who art in Heaven." The answer is what we refer to as the Lord's Prayer, a prayer presented, not as a manner of how to approach God, not as a manner of how to speak to God, but as a manner of how to live life. Jesus has given the Lord's Prayer not as a technique, but as a paradigm for how to live fully conscious, completely awake, wholly with God, in the new wine of the Spirit. It is to this pattern we now turn our attention.

Intimacy

The disciples asked, "How shall I pray?" This is no longer our question; now we ask, "How shall I live?" To both of these questions Jesus delivers the same initial response: "Our Father who art in Heaven..." Here is our first intention. The beginning of our daily life is a realization that we already have a fully established, intimate relationship with God.

Life is about this intimacy and relationship. It is upon this foundation that all other aspects of the spiritual life will be built. We begin to attune ourselves to the realization that it is God's passionate desire to have a truly intimate relationship with us. We also recognize that by God's own energy and gift, tenderness and affection are already present. The mystics may call it union or the Beatific Vision, the lover may know it as an embrace, but by whatever name or experience it is perceived, it is the intention and meaning of life; to be so close to God that we come to realize our identity in him. This is why Jesus begins by telling us that prayer is something between us and God alone. We are to go into our room and shut the door and meet the Father in secret. It is about our individual intimacy with God.

Most approaches to the spiritual life address the manner by which we might find God. They are about the correct manner of searching for God. The appropriate method of invocation or calling upon God, so that He will answer, so that he will respond. Jesus begins where these approaches end. Jesus tells us that the beginning of the spiritual life and of every prayerful utterance, is the recognition that God already is ours to have and be with. He does not instruct us to call out, "Where are you, Father? Come to me, I am in dire need of your presence." He does not teach us to take on the attitude of a groveler who cries out to God, "Just let me be the lowest servant in your house!" However useful these thoughts may be to produce a level of humility in an otherwise prideful person, this is not the heart of Jesus' direction. Rather, he posits a more friendly approach: he tells us to assume that we are already the beloved child of an ever-present, ever-loving father. "Our Father": these words imply an already existing condition. It is not, "O Almighty, distant, and uncaring God, please look on me and accept me," but, in the words of Jesus, the innocent cry of "Daddy".

Those who had fathers who loved them, doted upon them and wanted to be with them know well the feeling. For those who had distant, absent, or otherwise difficult fathers, this may be the first time in life that they begin to experience this feeling. Whatever the case, this is the feeling that Jesus offers as the starting point of each life, for every moment of life. It is the understanding that Jesus would later express in his story we now call the parable of the Prodigal Son.

As we recall the story[13], there was a father and two sons, one of whom did what his father seemed to value and the other who was selfish and ungrateful. The selfish, ungrateful son demands his inheritance money from the father and takes off to join in the devilment of the world. Of course, as is often the case, he loses all his money in attempts to find and sustain fleeting happiness and pleasure, only to end inexorably in degradation, loneliness, and want. He decides to return home and plead with his father to give him a job. He would not even think of asking for love or caring, only for the favor of a lowly service job in the family business so that he can survive. His father—to the son's surprise—does not even let him finish his plea. There is no need for making his son grovel for a few vengeful moments, no desire that the son must pay for what he has done before he can be accepted. His father just embraces him heartily.

This is true confession, true repentance, true forgiveness and love. To turn and go back to the father is repentance. To go back home is confession. So too with God. For us, saying *yes* means

---

we have turned back to God, turned our back on the false ways of life, the false identities we have created. This is confession and repentance: saying yes to God. If we will take a moment to listen and feel, God responds before all the groveling words can come out of our mouths. He embraces us and clothes us in Himself.

Unfortunately, is it not true that we still come to God with the attitude of the prodigal son? Do we not, even after two millennia of having this story told to us—even after all of these years of saying the Lord's Prayer—continue to pray like the son: "I am unworthy, please just let me be in your household as the lowest". We often painstakingly continue with this attitude; and all the while Jesus is telling us that God—like the father of the story—is waiting with open arms to embrace us in the greatest intimacy. That may be why it is so difficult for us to believe that salvation and the wholeness of life come with our simple yes to God. It seems naive and unsophisticated to think that the God of the universe can be attained merely by saying "I believe" and turning to him. But that famous scripture, "For God so loved that world that he gave his only Son that any who would believe in him should be saved,"[14] means exactly what it says. God loves, and now he asks us to embrace him. We are merely to say yes. He has the house and provision awaiting us. It is done. It really is as simple as that, if only we accept it.

Every prayer, every moment of the spiritual life, every moment of all of our lives is to begin with the acknowledgment of this simple yet profound truth: God has already provided the intimate relationship, now we need merely accept it. This is partially what it means to be as a little child. What child is not shocked if their mother and father are not accepting of them and will not be there for them? It is what is so confounding for the child whose parents are aloof and rejecting. Love and acceptance is expected, and if it is not shown then the child is disturbed and dumbfounded. As we accept God as Father, we can be as naïve as the child who just knows the presence and love of her or his parent.

---

[14] John 3:16

In such a fatherly way, we are to know that God is, and is present. As we awaken in the morning our first thought may be this; as we travel through the day, this can be our thought; as we make a decision and ask for God's guidance, this is our starting point, and as we retire to sleep we do so in the knowledge that God is cradling us in his arms, and meeting us even in depths of the night.

Do we experience, recall, seek that intimacy at all moments? This is what it means to pray without ceasing. We live with the awareness of ever-present intimacy. Still, since it has been obviously difficult for many to accept and experience this, it may be legitimately asked, "how do I develop this?"

Like so many things in life, we have learned bad habits. One really bad habit is the false belief that God is far from us, and that we must earn his love. To undo many bad habits, especially those that incorporate bad beliefs, we must practice new habits and new ways of thinking. If you have developed the bad habit of drinking too much alcohol to deal with the stress of daily life, and have come to believe that a stiff nightcap is necessary to get a good night's sleep, then you must first realize that alcohol actually inhibits good sleep patterns. Afterwards you learn new daily coping skills and moderate the drinking.

Likewise, a spiritual bad habit is broken by new behaviors and thoughts. Whether it is in your prayerful approach to daily life, or preparing for a formal moment of meditation or prayer, we call upon a new thought: God is already gently and patiently waiting for us in each moment. In a time of formal meditation, concentrate on the single-minded knowledge that God is already present with you. Remain with this thought: God is here. If you find the old habit raising its head, and your thoughts turn to such things as, "Well I am saying God is here, so should I not be seeing or feeling him? But I don't, so I guess I must be doing something wrong," realize that this is merely the mind once again getting in the way of reality.

30

Minds think, that is their job. Let it think what it may, but gently return to the sole thought, "God is here." If you find yourself asking for God to reveal Himself, then once again recognize the action of the mind that you have let yourself slip back into the belief that God has not revealed Himself and needs to do so. Gently remind yourself that it is not God's lack of presence or revelation but our blindness that is the problem, that such has been your bad habit and former belief.

Then, merely refocus on the reality that God is already here, even saying out loud with a knowing tone, as if speaking to someone you see in front of you, "my true loving Father", because this is where it all begins, this is where formal prayer and meditation commence, this is where our daily life launches out: "Our Father…"

The Fullness of Life

We have asked the searching question: "How am I to live a truly spiritual life?" The transforming response has come from Jesus, a response we have learned to call The Lord's Prayer. Jesus began by saying, "O Father, Who art in Heaven..." This is the open secret of the Christian life, the message that initiates our entry into true life: knowing that God is as intimate with us as a good Father, waiting to share life with us, and like so many fathers, wanting to pass on good gifts to his children; and, if they will allow, hoping that they will follow in his footsteps. Intimacy is the opening to this profound life, and it is profound. However, most of us have found it challenging to articulate exactly what it is that we are seeking. We may feel it in our hearts, but the mind has difficulty grasping words to describe this desire. It seems as if it is up to the poets and artists to express it for us. However, there is a story which reveals some of the answer. It is the story of a man who also came to Jesus asking just such a question, "How can I gain eternal life?"[15]

Jesus and the disciples often traveled between villages. It was at one such time that a young man came in search of Jesus; seeing an opportunity, he came to ask Jesus a question. This man was unlike many of Jesus' followers. He was one who appeared to have it all: money, a good education, likely coming from a good family. We also know that he probably was not a person given over to addictions and debauchery, as he would later tell Jesus that he had been leading an upright religious life according to the Jewish custom and laws. What is odd is that, to an outside observer, this is the type of life that most envy. What kind of need could have compelled him to search out Jesus?

Many of us think that if we had enough money to feel secure, if we just had good friends, a good church, and sufficient

---

[15] Matthew 19:16

time for some fun, that life would be just fine. Not so for our young man. He was not satisfied with life. Something inside him told him life was to have more zest. Then he heard of the excitement that surrounded this prophetic preacher. "Maybe this man might have an answer for my tedium," he may have thought. "Maybe he could point me in the right direction."

This young man grabbed his opportunity and asked Jesus, "What do I need to do to gain eternal life?" Jesus first inquired about the prerequisite for the journey, "Are you really interested in the reality of life?" "Are you attempting to pursue a life with God?" To this the young man responds, "Yes, I have done all that religion tells me to do, now I want more." As so often happened, Jesus could see this young man's heart and sees that he is ready for the step across the thin veil into real life. "Go, sell all you have, and come and be with me." After a dumbfounding moment, this sad young man merely walks away.

Material want, and grinding poverty are not things to be desired or valued. Once anyone has thought this through, who in their right mind would not walk away from such a demand? Who could follow such a teacher?

The problem is that this materialistic framing of the answer does not comprehend the spiritual reality to which Jesus was pointing. When we think of Jesus' answer in the terms of material objects we have missed the point. His answer is actually rather straightforward. Obviously, material objects and mere external activity have not been satisfying. If they had been the young man would not have been asking his question; so something needs to change. It is much like the old joke: a man walks into his doctor's office. The doctor asks "What is the problem?" The man lifts his arm above his head and says, "It hurts when I do this", to which the doctor responds, "Then stop doing it!" It is a simple joke that contains a great deal of wisdom. If something does not work, then stop doing it.

34

The definition of insanity (attributed to Albert Einstein) is "doing the same thing over and over again, expecting a different result". When the young man tells Jesus that he has all the opportunities that a wealthy life can offer, and that he has lived an externally diligent religious life, Jesus (like any good diagnostician) offers a commonsense prescription: stop doing what you have been doing and do something different. Stop living a predominately externalized life and enter into the joys of the inner life.

To us this now seems obvious. What we find satisfying in life is to live with a sense of purpose. It is to have relationships of deep affection and love; to know that our lives have meaning, and—in essence—to become the full person God destined each of us to be. All of these qualities—meaning, purpose, affection, love, and an inner harmonious life—are qualities of the inner life. Our external activities are products of these qualities, they are neither their origin nor their essence. So it is that Jesus is pointing this young man and us in the direction of deep satisfaction: embracing the inner life.

We legitimately may ask, "How do we set out to live this more satisfying, inner life?" We begin by knowing our goal. Few of us have taken vacations, or gone on journeys, with no goal in mind. Rather, most of us establish a goal, giving a sense of direction and purpose to what we are doing. Few of us when asked, "Where are you going on vacation?" will answer, "I am just getting in the car and driving." Or, if a student in university is asked what they are studying and they answer "I have no idea," they might be seen as misguided. Goals determine the direction of the paths taken.

It is the goal of entering into God's holiness that Jesus next presents in the Lord's Prayer when he says, "Our Father, who art in Heaven, hallowed be Thy name." After realizing the intimacy of God as Father, we are now to recognize that God is Holy.

To many of us this may seem obvious; however, holiness is not actually all that well understood. In articulating the meaning of holiness we end up with a circular definition. We say that if something is godly then it is holy. But then we say that God is holy. Finally, attempting to escape this endlessly wheel, we just say, "holiness means to be good". But this merely begs the question and oversimplifies a profound issue.

What is holiness? The simplest answer to this is that holiness is similar to wholeness. With this in mind we can understand that God is the fullness of all reality. Since God is holy then all joy, all satisfaction, all knowledge (of self and otherwise), all meaning, all purpose, all everything, is found in God. Here the meaning of God as holy is that in God is found all fulfillment and all completion. In Him is the beginning and end of everything.

If we want a full and meaningful life then it must begin and end in Him who is all fullness and meaningfulness. If we want pleasure and satisfaction, then it must begin and end in the place where all pleasure and satisfaction find their fulfillment. God is holy; if I wish to find my soul's inner concord, if I want the internal chorus—alluded to earlier—to sing in harmony, it must begin and end in my uniting with God. When I truly—that is experientially—realize that all I seek in life is found in the fullness of God, then God's holiness presents a claim on my very being, and I turn completely toward God.

This is what Jesus wants his hearers to understand. This is what he hoped that the young man in the story would grasp. Nothing can get in the way of pursuing God. This is what it may mean to understand that God is a jealous God. He desires the same intimacy that we unconsciously desire, and He wants for us the same wholeness and harmony to which we unconsciously feel called. He does not want anything to come between us and our destiny together. Nothing is to get in the way; sell it all, submit everything that might distract from the true pursuit. When we do, we finally encounter the feeling we have so desired: we come into contact with the numinous.

This word "numinous" was coined by the theologian Rudolph Otto in 1928, and presented in his seminal book, *The Idea of the Holy*.[16] Otto found the need for a word which he could use for an experience of something that was completely beyond our comprehension, since the word holiness—which once carried the meaning—had now been relegated to the exclusive meaning of goodness.

Earlier in history, holiness had a grander connotation. When one encountered the holy it could be in the ethical sense of goodness, but just as likely could describe the ethically difficult encounter with a wildly dangerous god, such as the dark side of the Hindu goddess Kali, the Yahweh who sent an evil spirit upon Saul, or even a Dionysus overcoming and possessing the passions of a person. Holiness was that moment, that experience of something so beyond the ordinary that it could take your breath away and not only your breath, but also your words. Most of us have had the experience in a dream of encountering something (often very fearful) that was so overwhelming that no words would come, no scream could sound. Those dreams are very disconcerting, but they are mere indications of the silence that often accompanies the numinous.

Silence is one aspect of the numinous often mentioned in the mystic encounter. The experience of the encounter is often portrayed in art as the feeling one obtains from perceiving darkness or semi-darkness, a sensation described in Genesis as being with God as he walked with them in the cool of the day[17]; or the darkness utilized by Caravaggio in his biblical paintings; utilizing distance and void to express this mood. Likewise, silence is often the paradoxical experience of the numinous, as is illustrated in the subtitle of Jeffrey Burton Russell's informative book *A History of*

[16] Otto, Rudolph (1958). The Idea of the Holy, Oxford Univ. Press, Oxford.
[17] cf. Genesis 3:8

Heaven: The Singing Silence[18]. Darkness, void, silence, these are all the experiences of the mystic encountering the holiness of God.

This may be why silence is such an important a part of encountering the reality of God. So often scripture pleads with us to be silent[19], and to "be still and know that I am God."[20] Once we realize that God is the fullness of all life and that He is ever present and waiting for us in embracing intimacy, then we find ourselves willingly giving ourselves to him.

The next words almost flow automatically from our lips, "Thy Kingdom come, Thy will be done..." This is the beginning of the full, unconditional surrender of the ego to the deeper realms of the self, and to Him who is all in all, desiring to hold back nothing. The little fish in our vast ocean now finds itself so attracted to the reality that is beyond it, that submission to the deeper self, and all joy and darkness such an activity embodies, is worth the effort and the pain merely to touch the numinous.

When we come into the presence of such wonder, into the presence of such satisfying relationship, such fullness, our hearts begin to swell. When this happens in human love, we find that just being with our beloved is more than sufficient, words are unnecessary. To gaze upon one another in silent wonder is like drinking in the other. In such moments words fail, words may even break the spell. It is a time for silent wonder, a moment that accompanies the recognition of being in the presence of all we seek. This is the miraculous moment of being fully enveloped in reality, with the masks and falseness that dominate our lesser moments stripped away. This is what it is like to sit in silent wonder, in the intimacy of the affection found with God. It may be why silence is the favored mode of the mystic who strives with almost panicked desire to reach that silence where God is to be

---

[18] Russell, Jeffey Burton (1997). <u>A History of Heaven: The Singing Silence</u>. Princeton University Press.
[19] cf. Zephaniah 1:7 "Be silent before the Lord GOD!"
[20] Psalm 46:10

fully enjoyed. The poet and theologian John O'Donahue said it this way:

> Meister Eckhart said that nothing in the universe resembles God so much as silence, so if you think about silence in that sense, then to come into silence is to come into the presence of the Divine. In a way, you allow yourself to be enfolded by that stillness. In a real sense, the deepest thing in a human heart is not the verbage but is actually that still silence—not the silence of Buddhism, which often seems to me maybe something anonymous—but is the silence of intimacy where no word is needed and where a word would actually be a fracture.[21]

The foundation of the spiritual life is now established. It is solidly placed upon the experience of an intimate embrace with God, a God who is waiting patiently and expectantly for us, like a Father awaiting the birth of his child; like a Father anticipating the joy of participating in the life and development of his offspring. A foundation of experiencing the completeness of all that is searched for is laid while we are silently opening our hearts to the presence of Him who is all fullness and all reality. To submit to the embrace of such a reality is to open one's heart to life. This is the ground of a deep life, a life that flows from the cry of our hearts: "Our Father, who art in heaven, You alone are holy and all is to be found in You alone. So may Your kingdom come, Your will be done, on earth as it always has been in heaven."

---

[21] O'Donahue, John (2015). Walking on the Pastures of Wonder. Veritas Press, Dublin.

Provision for the Journey

For the person making any important life decision, determining the will of God is vital. For the man or woman who cares about the afterlife, searching for the will of God is imperative. Merely the desire to live a healthy, full, and effective life entails a search for this will. All of these make knowing the will of God a task of immeasurable urgency. So much time and energy is expended by well-meaning people attempting to determine the will of God and it seems like such a daunting task, when really it is not as difficult as it is made out to be; that is, when approached in the manner presented by Jesus in the Lord's Prayer.

The almost panicked search for the will of God takes on a different perspective in the mind of the German mystic Meister Eckhart. John O'Donahue says this about Eckhart and the will of God.

> "In one of his beautiful Latin sermons, Eckhart says that 'in the first glance of God, everything that is in the world was born'. It is a very artistic notion of the divine imagination. An awful lot of theology and spirituality goes badly to ground in an excessive concentration on the will of God— poor humans trying to beat their lovely complex minds into the direction of that will—whereas Meister Eckhart tries to awaken you to the divine imagination and to help you realize that that is where you have come from, that is what holds you together in the world, that is where your ultimate destination is."[22]

Eckhart is saying that we are conceived in the mind of God; the prophet Jeremiah says for God, "I knew you before you were conceived in the womb"[23]. Michelanglo portrayed it so beautifully

---

[22] O'Donahue, John (2015). <u>Walking on the Pastures of Wonder</u>. Veritas, Dublin

[23] Jeremiah 1:5

in the Sistene Chapel where we find Eve and all of future humanity in the waves of God's garment, waves that appear in the shape of a brain. It is by means of the continued imagining by God that we exist moment-by-moment—both Job and Isaiah allude to the fact that every breath depends on the grace of God; and it is through His imagination of who we are that we are destined. Instead of demanding that we strive to know the will of God, Jesus may be more interested in us uniting with this divine imagination; in our truly embracing God.

In the Lord's Prayer, Jesus has shown the way of flowing in God's will. It is what we have been discussing in the initial aspects of this prayer. As we embrace the intimacy of God and allow ourselves to be enveloped in His fullness—that which we call His holiness—we become one with the imagination of God. In that act, we do not merely know the will of God, we become it.

However, in our ego's desire to remain independent and in control of its own privately conceived destiny, it subtly distracts us from our true vocation by having us search for an abstract "will of God' which is still separate from our life, somehow outside of it. It demands that we continue to view God as distant and aloof. In such a situation, the will of God can only remain obscure.

Jesus points us in a different direction. He directs us to a nearer God into whose life and imagination we are invited. We are taught, "O Father in heaven, your name is holy." When we experience that friendship and that fullness, the kingdom has come into our souls and God's will is simply a consequence of that experience. It is no longer the beating of our lovely complex minds, nor a hearty striving to understand, it is merely a result of living as Jesus has called us to live. As we stop trying find out how to please God and start gently being with him, we no longer work to know God's will: we become it.

An apt illustration of this reality is the life of St. David of Wales. David was one of those blessed souls who early on knew he wanted to live a true life. As a child he enjoyed the stories of God and took to learning the ways of God with vigor. As a teenager and adult he sought out others who desired to know God and enjoyed learning and being with them. Later, he gathered a few of these hearty souls and together they moved to a remote hollow on the Pembrokeshire coast of Wales.

It was a good location for a number of reasons. It afforded solitude and safety. This was especially important a few centuries later, because by establishing themselves near the coast, the marauding Vikings could possibly have attacked and destroyed them, as they did Iona and so many other monasteries. However, by placing themselves in a valley, they remained unseen from the sea and the Vikings sailed by, leaving them unmolested. This valley also reflected God's beauty in nature and the elements. Even today it is a favored vacation spot for Londoners wishing a bit of something more natural than sidewalks and fumy undergrounds. David and his soul friends would live the devout life there in that corner of Britain which today bears his name.

Their life was spent in intense periods of inner silence; chanting of Psalms; and vocal prayer vigorously mixed with physical labor and the study of the Scriptures. All life was a mental, spiritual, and physical consecration to God. David was one who embodied and en-souled embracing the intimacy of God with the reality of finding all that is of value in that divine friendship. Because of this, when the time came for him to lead others, the wisdom and will of God would beautifully shine forth from him.

There was a period throughout these early centuries of Christianity—we are speaking here of the sixth century—when the newly minted orthodoxy would be challenged. People throughout Britain had once again begun to embrace a belief that if they could just be good enough, they would attain the glories of heaven. It was an old belief, one that had been rejected in favor of the understanding that what was impossible for humans alone ("being good enough") could only be accomplished by the Spirit of Jesus, and it was only by being enveloped in his life that the glories of heaven were to be entered. The old belief had taken a strong hold on the land, so a synod was gathered. All of the bishops and clergy had come to Wales to argue the point, but no one was able to win the day. The British Church stood on the edge of disaster when some inspired soul reminded the orthodox present that the holy man, David, had not come to the gathering. They all agreed they needed to hear from him and in unison called for David to be consulted and for him to come and speak.

David had little love for such debates and initially withdrew from the invitation. He considered that such debates only tended to draw one's mind and soul from the glories of God and into a world of pride and rancor. He wanted only to experience God's life, not to be a great theologian. However, after much persuasion, he accompanied those who implored him and arrived at the synod.

As is typical with theological debates, everyone was speaking and no one was listening. Each was attempting to establish their point, often relishing the brilliance of their own words. Then David began to speak. Of course, no one heard him through the cacophony of self-promotion.

This was when the miracle happened. Suddenly, the ground rose under David's feet so that all saw him standing on a small hill, a hill upon which the church of Llandewi Breifi stands to this day in honor of this moment. This silenced the crowd. But then something not so miraculous—not miraculous because we are pointing out that this is the natural result of such a life—but astounding all the same, occurred. The crowd witnessed a white dove descend from the sky and alight upon the shoulder of David. Turning to him, it put its beak to his ear as if whispering.

David spoke words so profound, a wisdom so deep, that none would contend with him and the cacophony was silenced. The day had been won in favor of orthodoxy and of Christ's atonement. Later, David would be consecrated by the Patriarch of

44

Jerusalem as Archbishop of the British Isles. However, his desire was constantly to remain in silence and listening prayer, the singing of Psalms, and finding his joy in God alone. Because of this, the will and wisdom of God would shine forth from him.

When we follow his example, we become the very will of God, and we also live in the presence and flow of the Spirit. We live in the reality of the Kingdom of Heaven, the Kingdom within. But the fullness of the New Creation, the Kingdom of Heaven manifest outside our soul, is not yet completely experienced. So another question is now raised and immediately answered by Jesus: "How do we maintain our relationship with God throughout the days ahead?" "With the pressures of this outer world, how do we maintain the presence of the Kingdom within?" Jesus' answer: "Give us this day our daily bread." Knowing the need to address this concern, Jesus teaches us to now call upon God for this sustaining power, this continuing nourishment of the Kingdom within.

This portion of the Lord's Prayer is, in many ways, likely the most familiar. At first glance it appears to teach us about reaching out to God in order to meet our needs and those of others in the outer world. The plea of the disciples was "Teach us to pray", the same request that so many of us utter in times of need. We are in need. We, and others are sick: we need healing. There is injustice all around; we call for righteousness. Finances are always an issue, please supply our needs. But how are we to correctly request all of these things? How does one appropriately ask God for provision? How does one properly speak to God? So the request: "Please, teach us to pray."

As we ponder the depth of Jesus' response, we hear the echos of other answers. A frequent reply is to view prayer as a simple conversation with God. When taught to pray the advice is given to just start talking to God as you would to anyone else. This is clear, simple advice, but like so much clear simple advice it is easy to offer, but hard to do. When such advice is given it is assumed that conversation with others is easy, so just talk to God. For some, however, conversation is a mystery.

Having sat with lonely people, you know how difficult conversation can be for some. Well-intentioned acquaintances will often give lonely people advice to take a class, join a club, or go to church to make new friends. But for the lonely, the question still lingers, "I go to the class, but then what do I do?" Often he or she merely sits invisibly in the class and leaves without speaking to anyone else. At a meeting or party, they wonder how to begin and sustain a conversation; and without the answer, they remain alone in the crowd. It is hopelessness that seems to be reinforced by these well-intentioned efforts. If it is this difficult to talk with people who are, as yet, of little significance, how much more difficult it can be with God to whom is attributed great significance, and with whom you want to get the conversation right. This difficulty in talking to God becomes even more pronounced since God often seems to talk softly and with such long pauses.

At the party, the person who does not know what to talk about but forces themselves into a moment of extraversion, often falls back on merely talking about themselves, which then turns to talking about their problems, which then creates another barrier. Who wants to share their depths with someone they are meeting for the first time?

When it comes to social situations there is a good piece of advice that often works that may also work in prayer as well; have a few good questions ready that prompt the other person to talk about themselves. Get the other person to do most of the talking. People often like to talk about themselves more than listen. The principle is the same for God. Allow Him to do most of the talking, which implies that we do more of the listening.

We may not have a list of good questions to ask God, however it is silence in the presence of God that works best.

Unfortunately, this is not commonly how our times with God take place. More often these times take a nervous turn toward awkward party conversations, with us filling in the silence with all of our problems and concerns. It may be for this reason that prayer is so frequently dominated by requests for God's help. But when these run out, we are left not knowing what to say. So we stop with a hasty "Amen". When told that someone else might spend an hour or two in prayer, have you ever wondered, "What on earth do they have to say for that long?" It is a common thought, and one that belies that fact that we think we have to do all the talking both in prayer and with others.

When the bulk of prayer is comprised of our expressing a need for this or that, then the result is often the same as the lonely party-goer; we leave the prayer time more hopeless than when we began, because (if we are honest with ourselves) most of our prayers seem to go unanswered. We then struggle on in a form of denial, still praying, but not really believing it is of much worth; still we go through the motions because somewhere deep within we still harbor the hope that one time it may work.

This is quite evident when we get really excited over a real miracle. Since we prayed for it, should not it have been expected to happen? However, when prayer does seem to work we see it and exclaim "I can't believe it, look at what happened!" then run around telling anyone who will listen about the extraordinary event: a prayer was answered! More common is our tendency to identify with the role of the mourners at the death of Jairus' daughter.[24]

Jairus' daughter was on the verge of death. In desperation, this religious leader goes to seek out the itinerant preacher Jesus in hope that he might keep his daughter from death. By the time he arrives back home with Jesus the girl has died. Surrounding the house are the mourners, praying for the family and doing the religious thing. This is where we need to be careful because we cannot easily condemn the mourners. They are leading what might

---

[24] Luke 8:41ff; Mark 5:22ff

47

be considered good, godly lives. They are praying to God and they are performing the correct actions. The problem lies with their attitude, it is all wrong as they display with their scoffing.

Jesus proclaims that the girl will not remain dead but will live. The gathering scoffs in disbelief. They know better than to ask for something so ridiculous as making dead girls live. But at the word of Jesus she will live. Jesus does not wish for us to follow the manner of mourning crowd, but for us adopt the attitude of Jairus, and attitude of expectation. He asked Jesus for something and Jesus said yes. That is enough. This is the essence of all petitions: does Jesus say yes?

To know whether Jesus is saying yes or no does not flow out of seeking his will but being in his will. It flows out of the foundational relationship. What is such a struggle for many now becomes second nature; when you are in that essential relationship you just know, intuitively. Some call it discernment, but it is no different than being in a boat on a flowing river. There is no way of not knowing the direction of the current, just try rowing in any other direction and you will discover it. When in that intimate, desired relationship, we flow with God's current. All it takes is enough silence and enough courage to look within, and it is experienced.

We spend a great deal of time determining what we and others need and then figuring out how to get God to respond appropriately. The way Jesus teaches it, our energy is better invested in determining what God wants and flowing in that. God already knows our needs and those of others and merely needs our participation in the fulfilling. This may be why the Lord's Prayer spends such little energy on petitions and intercessions, arguably even no time! As we will soon observe, the seeking of daily bread may have little or nothing to do with provision of our mundane needs.

It is an interesting fact that most of our prayers are taken up requesting provision: food, shelter, money, health, and the like. To see these in the Lord's Prayer takes a bit of squeezing; they almost have to be artificially inserted into Jesus' teaching on prayer. Jesus teaches that we are to expend energy in seeking a deepened relationship with God and that provisions flow from that. In this regard, the act we think of as meditation is central to the prayer life, while vocal prayers of need are secondary. We see this in the Lord's Prayer as Jesus further explains it during the Sermon on the Mount. There he again says:

> [D]o not be anxious about your life, what you will eat or what you will drink, nor about your body, what you will put on. Is not life more than food, and the body more than clothing? Look at the birds of the air: they neither sow nor reap nor gather into barns, and yet your heavenly Father feeds them. Are you not of more value than they? And which of you by being anxious can add a single hour to his span of life? And why are you anxious about clothing? Consider the lilies of the field, how they grow: they neither toil nor spin, yet I tell you, even Solomon in all his glory was not arrayed like one of these. But if God so clothes the grass of the field, which today is alive and tomorrow is thrown into the oven, will he not much more clothe you, O you of little faith? Therefore do not be anxious, saying, 'What shall we eat?' or 'What shall we drink?' or 'What shall we wear?' For the Gentiles seek after all these things, and your heavenly Father knows that you need them all. But seek first the kingdom of God and his righteousness, and all these things will be added to you. Therefore do not be anxious about tomorrow, for tomorrow will be anxious for itself. Sufficient for the day is its own trouble.[25]

Here, with even more startling clarity, Jesus teaches the way of prayer. Relax, enter into the intimate silence of a relationship with God, experience the fullness and satisfaction of that

---

[25] Matthew 6:25ff

relationship; seek first the Kingdom. Then you will just know by inner experience the will of God—how could you not, you are bathed in it—and all your needs will be met. Of course, that will mean the needs of your whole self, not those only conceived by the ego, nor those that are directed in fulfilling a mundane, transitory life.

What we have observed so far is that the foundation of the spiritual life is set in the intimacy and fullness of our relationship to God. The things of the mundane life flow from this. We ask, because it is a natural part of our relationship. In relationships we ask and give, give and ask.

James, the first bishop of Jerusalem, knew this. He said in his letter found in the New Testament, "You do not have, because you do not ask. You ask and do not receive, because you ask wrongly, to spend it on your passions."[26] God is not some impersonal force that we can manipulate as is taught in certain pseudo-philosophies such as the "laws of attraction" or prosperity theologies. God is a person who relates and calls us to relate back. But when we ask with only an interest of getting and not with the desire for relationship, then the asking seems to fall flat. What we are to do is to speak like the child asking his or her parent "what is for dinner?" The child's question is not *if* there will be dinner, but what *is* for dinner. It is expected, it is merely a matter of relaxing and patiently waiting for what already is prepared.

Jesus is teaching us to relax, mundane provision will be there for us. It is rather an odd thing, then, that we should be taught to plead for it daily ("Give us this day our daily bread") as if God might somehow forget. Knowing that God is not some demented soul, so forgetful that he needs constant reminding, demands that we look at this request for daily bread in another, deeper, manner.

---

[26] James 4:2

The unveiling of an answer may be in the very phrase itself: "Give us this day our daily bread." Brant Pitre[27], in his study of the Jewish roots of the Last Supper, asks the provocative question, "why does Jesus repeat himself in this phrase?" Why not, "Give us this day our bread", or just "Give us our daily bread"? Why refer to the day twice? This is one of those places where a knowledge of the Greek language is helpful. What we find is that two different words are used in this phrase.

The first is based on the Greek word, *hemeron*, meaning this day as we commonly conceive of it. The second, the one translated daily bread, is *epiousion*. Now this is an interesting word. If we split it apart it become *epi* and *ousion*. *Ousion* is a Greek word for being or substance, while *epi* means upon or over, as in epithelium, or the skin that is over and above the remainder of the body. Epiousion has been difficult for Bible scholars as it is only used as such in this phrase of the Lord's Prayer. So they work the best they can with the context and default to a translation of "daily bread." But if we take the word at face value, then it would literally mean above-being, over-substance, or supernatural.

As we have just been exploring, for Jesus to place such importance in his short prayer on our asking for provision for our food seems incongruous. However, with his emphasis on our intimate relationship with God and our seeking of holiness, it is more reasonable to see that he now answers the question of how to attain and sustain that relationship. It is, in each moment and day of life, to ask for the supernatural bread: the manna of heaven. The Lord's Prayer might better be translated as "Give us this day our supernatural bread," the supernatural provision for a heavenly life lived this very day.

For many of us in this modern day, this phrase and understanding may be strange. For the Jew of the first century it would be a more familiar concept. The Jews at this time, and

[27] Pitre, Brant (2011). The Jewish Roots of the Eucharist. Ignatius Press. San Francisco

subsequently, associated the coming of the Messiah with a new revelation of the heavenly manna. Pitre tells us that the Jews held three interesting traditions about the manna.

First, the manna existed from the beginning of creation. In the Pseudo-Jonathan Targum on Exodus 16:4 (a translation of the Hebrew Scriptures used in the synagogue) we read:

> And the Lord said to Moses, "Behold, I will bring down for you bread from heaven, which has been reserved for you from the beginning."

And then a few verses later:

> When the children of Israel saw [it], they were amazed and said to one another, "What is it?" For they did not know what it was. And Moses said to them, "It is the bread that was reserved for you from the heavens on high; and now the Lord is giving it to you to eat. (16:15)

Another tradition common at the time was that the manna was kept in the temple of God in the heaven of heavens. As is alluded to in the Letter to the Hebrews, the Jews (in an echo of Plato) saw things on earth as shadows of the real that were in the heaven of heavens. Things on earth were a type, a reflection, of the archetype in heaven. So, in the earthly temple in Jerusalem (as in the tabernacle of the Exodus) inside the Ark of the Covenant would be stored the staff of Aaron, the tablets of the Covenant, and a jar of the manna. This was to reflect that in the heaven of heavens the real manna was in the holy of holies of God's real presence.

Pitre then tells us of the third tradition that impacts our reading of the Lord's Prayer. He says:

> The third Jewish tradition about the manna that is important for us flows directly from the second. Since the

rabbis believed that the manna continued to exist in heaven, even after it ceased on earth, many of them were waiting for the manna to return one day. And since they also believed that the Messiah would be a new Moses, many of them expected that the return of the manna would take place at the coming of the Messiah.[28]

Knowing this, it is easier for us to grasp Jesus' many references to himself as the Bread of Life. He was continually referring to these rabbinic traditions, as well as adding to them. For he was now identifying himself with that manna.

The manna is the supernatural food that sustained people on their journey from mundane slavery to the glory of the Promised Land. It tasted sweet, like honey, carrying in it the food of the future (the land of milk and honey). So Jesus brings the renewed manna, the food that takes us from the slavery of this diminishing creation, sustaining us on our journey to the fullness of the New Creation, the consummated Kingdom of God. It sustains us with food of that consummation, the life of God himself, given within us. This was the teaching on the Eucharist that Jesus was presenting to his disciples at the Last Supper, prefigured in the dialogues recorded in the sixth chapter of the Gospel of John, and hinted at in the Lord's Prayer. "Give us each day the manna of the New Creation." As you gave our forefathers manna to sustain them on their way to the Promised Land on this earth, give us the heavenly manna to sustain us as we traverse this world looking to enter eternity in the New Creation. "Give us this day our supernatural bread."

Later, at the Last Supper, Jesus was to bring down this manna. It is fascinating to realize that the focus of the Gospel accounts is not the Pascal Lamb, as you might expect, but the bread. At that moment Jesus would bring down this manna, now identified with His body, and He would reiterate his advice in the Lord's Prayer, "every time you gather together, do this in

---

[28] ibid.

remembrance of me", give us every time we are together your life to sustain us.

The basis of our daily life is now set. We are prepared. We encounter God with the knowledge of His patient, intimate love and desire for us. In that dance, we experience the Kingdom of God; it has truly come into the world and into the depths or our hearts. In those depths the will of God is manifest, and because we listen we are intuitively led into the will and way of God. We recognize and experience that all that our souls could ever desire is found in the fullness of divine friendship, and that out of that fullness even our mundane demands are met. The true life is sustained in the miraculous feeding of our souls by the heavenly manna: Jesus himself in the Eucharist.

Our Father, who art in heaven, hallowed by thy name, thy Kingdom come, thy will be done on earth as if is in Heaven. Give us this day our daily bread.

Now we are prepared to deal with community, and taught how to live with others: Forgiveness.

Forgiveness

From the outset of his teaching on prayer, Jesus emphasizes the quality of our relationship with God. Many know this but overlook it in practice. For others, God is the eternal strategist playing a chess match with an opponent who some say is Satan and others merely some anonymous opponent. People are the various pieces. The famous are the powerful pieces, such a bishop, queen, or knight. The remainder of us are sacrificial pawns. We may say that God is interested in us individually, however our behavior and attitudes belie the belief that we are merely here to serve a purpose in the pursuit of some cosmic victory in God's game. This has led many people to batter their "complex little minds" into shape attempting to determine God's next move for them, and what "service" they should be performing. This concept finds no basis in Jesus' prayer.

Nowhere in the Lord's Prayer can we find a place where Jesus says, "teach us this day what service we are supposed to perform, what evangelistic work we are to do, what mission we are to go on." However, these too often are the questions that we ask ourselves and others.

Someone comes to a church and as soon as they indicate their desire to grow deeper with God they are questioned about what ministry they may like to perform. It is not that such questions are not important; they are. It is rather that such questions are secondary and not of first concern. The first question to be asked is, "How is your inner relationship with God?"

Frequently I am asked how one begins in spiritual direction. What does one do? In psychotherapy a person approaches the work with a problem or something troubling enough to compel them to enter the work. Spiritual direction is different, there often is no problem. The approach to beginning spiritual formation is to ponder the question, "Who is God to me?" This is what Jesus proposes when he teaches that prayer starts with the intimate relationship between you and God and continues with the fullness of the life to be attained and the manner of sustaining that offered life. Once the grounding of life with God is established, then answers to the questions of service and outer activities merely present themselves, as does the answer to determining the will of God. Service and activity to the community flow peacefully from our God-grounded hearts.

The post-modern world is a culprit in developing a domineering technological attitude which even the Church has adopted by osmosis. The post-modern world asks different questions and has a different focus than does the divine. The world proposes questions framed by *what* and *how*. God asks *who*. In our modern and post-modern emphasis on external achievement the question of who you are is lost in the morass of what you are, what you do, and how you do it. We have been overcome by a technological mentality that is destroying the individual.

Even though we obviously value this post-modern mentality (we certainly enjoy its material benefits) our souls know the danger, a danger that has taken on mythic proportions. Merely witness the fascination with such films as *The Matrix, Terminator,* and *Star Wars.* Each of these films is an obvious statement of technology usurping one's humanity and the fight to regain our humanity. In a more covert manner it is also the theme of J.R.R. Tolkien's, *The Lord of the Rings.* It is well-known that Tolkien was no advocate of the mechanized life, seeing it as destroying humanity, something he witnessed firsthand in the fields of the First World War. His orcs are the deformed product of such technology, beautiful elves ruined by such evil.

Technology is developed and run by the *what* and the *how*. Purposes, goals, and methods are its way. When a technological mindset dominates then the value of life is defined by questions of what a person is, what a person does, and the discovery of how to attain goals. The manner in which Jesus talks about life, and the way that He teaches to pray, say that this is not His interest at all.

56

He is much more interested in the *who* of a person. Who are you? Who is God? Who is each of these other people around you? Who are you with God and others? These are the questions that matter. Not, what have you done for God? Nor, what have you done for others or they for you? *What* questions inhibit relationships, *who* questions build them.

It is an odd thing that in a society that appears so individualistic, even narcissistic, we have lost ourselves. In a society that has developed such wonderful means of mass communication, mobile phones, the internet, and the like, relationships have diminished. I would think that being able to call you at any time, to see your video presence on the internet while talking, by being able to get information in a flash, I would be more related to you and others. But the fact is that we only have the appearance of relationship; the depth is gone. We have devolved to the clipped sentences of X (former Twitter), the monologues of Facebook, and the sound bite of the media. Depth of the *who* has been sacrificed in favor of the shallow waters of the *what* and *how*.

It may not be so surprising to realize that, as the uniformity of the machine dominates our post-modern world, there is a growing level of narcissism. The psychologist will be able to see the reason for this, for narcissism is not really about the true, deep self, it is not about who I am, it is about what I am. As the society values what I am, the value of who I am diminishes. This is the heart of a narcissistic existence.

If we recall the metaphor of the ocean and the fish, the ocean being our psyche and the fish the ego, what we understand is that narcissism is the activity of the fish closing its eyes to all that is around it and being completely self-contained.

We often use the word narcissism in a broad way, frequently merely meaning selfish, or self-absorbed, or just self-centered. It is useful to see narcissism on a broader spectrum: at one end is the person who is acting selfishly and at the other end the person who knows nothing but his or her own ego-identity. Selfish people know they are being selfish, true narcissists do not quite get it that they are only focused on their own desires.

Many people who are at the far pole of ego-centered narcissism have become that way because of factors in their lives which have resulted in an inner world of pain. The waters directly around this little fish are polluted with rage, rejection, hopelessness, and despair. This has often been the result of exactly bathing in these emotions as small children.

A wonderful, but disturbing, book was written by the psychologist Alice Miller, *The Drama of the Gifted Child*.[29] She outlines many of the features found in the development of the narcissistic person. One of these features involved parents who wanted to create a perfect environment for their child so that the child could succeed. However, these same parents were so focused on success that they never truly loved the child's soul. These are the parents who take their children to the best resorts, and while there put them in wonderful day camps, never truly relating to the child. They send the child to the best schools, but do not know the depths of their hearts.

I recall overhearing a conversation while sitting at a small café near Boston. A man and woman were speaking with a young boy as he related his experiences in second grade discussing how he hoped third grade would be better. At first I thought him quite articulate, telling what seemed to be an interested aunt and uncle his experiences at this elite boarding school, only then to realize these were his parents. They showed real interest in his progress, but knew nothing of the boy's inner life. The result of such parenting is often outer world success, but an experience of inner relational rejection. No one ever touches their true life, and as an adult no one, not even their own ego, touches that deeper self. They become a *what* rather than a *who*, the result being that—right

---

[29] Miller, Alice (1979). The Drama of the Gifted Child. Basic Books. New York.

below the surface of consciousness—there is a reservoir of pain, rejection, hopelessness, despair, and of course rage. No wonder the fish closes its eyes, who would want to see and feel that, especially if you did not have to?

This is the problem with the narcissist, and with an overly technologically dominated society where success is determined by what you do rather than who you are; if you are successful in the outer life you effectively avoid this inner pain, at least for a time. But then you never get to truly live.

This can be seen in the lives of two recent Presidents of the United States: Bill Clinton and Barak Obama. Whether you agreed with their political stances or policies, what cannot be denied is that they were very successful; one does not become President of the United States without some grand measure of success. However, both of them appear very narcissistic. Interestingly, both have somewhat similar childhoods. Both of their fathers were absent. Both created idealized father images. President Clinton's biographers point to his idealization of John F. Kennedy, making him a form of father substitute. Barack Obama created an idealized image of a father as presented in his autobiography, *Dreams From My Father.*[30] However, both boys were groomed for outer, political, success while their hearts were neglected. Today, when forced to confront anything of the inner world—a confrontation that all of us face when others question our actions and motives—both respond with rage, rejection, and disbelief that others would so question them. These men are merely the tip of a societally sick iceberg created by valuing the *what* and *how* of people over the *who*.

Jesus calls us to the *who*. First, know who you are with God. When you begin to know who you are with God, then begin to know who you are with others. To do this we must value the *who* of God, the *who* of others, and the *who* of ourselves. If we thought the first portion of Jesus' teaching difficult, now we are walking upon the really challenging field. This is the field of self and other

---

[30] Obama, Barak (1995). <u>Dreams From My Father</u>. Crown Publ. Fort Collins.

discovery. Jesus gives us the way to traverse it; it is walked with the courage of forgiveness.

"Forgive us our trespasses as we forgive others their trespasses against us." This is how Jesus teaches us to reach out to the world about us. When we are offended by someone else we almost always frame our anger with words such as "What did you do?" or "How come you did that?" Our resentment and anger is often centered on the *what* and *how*. To circumvent this, we are taught to ask the *who* question. "Who is this that has done this?" Such a *who* demands that we touch the other's soul and begin to know them. Answers to the other questions of why something happened, what caused it to occur, how it transpired, all flow from this touching of souls. When souls touch, forgiveness has begun, because forgiveness is actually the re-establishing of a broken relationship.

An interesting fact is that relationship with God and others is not merely a privilege but is an expectation. That we would be in a full, loving relationship with God and with others is of such importance that it is framed in the terms of an essential obligation: it is what I owe God and others, and is reciprocally what is owed to me.

The Greek word used to convey what is to be forgiven is *opheiléma* which, when the King James version of the Bible was created, was best translated as trespass. Today we probably relate to it better as a debt. A debt is something that is owed, an obligation that is meant to be fulfilled. Jesus is teaching that as we relate to God and to others we must realize that all of us have an obligation and disturbingly that each of us will continue to fail in fulfilling this obligation.

The comforting part of this is that God knows that we are not perfect enough to follow through and does not hold our feet to the fire of being perfect. The whole sanctification process is initiated and assisted by God because we cannot accomplish it

60

alone. However, there is a catch: God wants us to be like him in this regard, not holding other people's feet to that fire either.

Our plea is something like, "I am not perfect, however I will do my best, but when I fail, please do not hold it against me I really do want to be completely a friend with you, God." Jesus tells us that if we have this attitude, then failure is not held against us. God remains much more interested in the *who* of me (I am imperfect) than the *what*. All that we are asked is to also be more concerned with the *who* of those other imperfect persons in our lives and not expect or demand flawlessness from them. If those that have hurt us desire to reestablish a real relationship—which is usually indicated by a sincere apology for a wrong—then it is to be accepted. Being in relationship with them is more important than having them fulfilling some transitory expectation or deed.

The warning is clear: make the soul of the other more important than their accomplishments. If your opinion is that people should never offend you, never fail you, always meet their obligations to you, then not only will you be sorely disappointed and likely filled with resentment and rage, but God and your own conscience will use these standards in dealing with you. "Judge not lest you be judged, the measure you use will be the measure used for you." This is not because God is vindictive and vengeful, but because it is a given of the unconscious that our outer attitude must be balanced by an equal inner attitude.

Jesus would expand on this. Within the Gospel of Matthew we find Peter asking Jesus about forgiveness. Jesus answered with a story.

The kingdom of heaven may be compared to a king who wished to settle accounts with his servants. When he began to settle, one was brought to him who owed him ten thousand talents. And since he could not pay, his master ordered him to be sold, with his wife and children and all that he had, and payment to be made. So the servant fell on his knees, imploring him, 'Have patience with me, and I will pay you everything.' And out of pity for him, the master of that servant released him and forgave him the debt. But when that same servant went out, he found one of his fellow servants who owed him a hundred denarii, and seizing him, he began to choke him, saying, 'Pay what you owe.' So his fellow servant fell down and pleaded with him, 'Have patience with me, and I will pay you.' He refused and went and put him in prison until he should pay the debt. When his fellow servants saw what had taken place, they were greatly distressed, and they went and reported to their master all that had taken place. Then his master summoned him and said to him, 'You wicked servant! I forgave you all that debt because you pleaded with me. And should not you have had mercy on your fellow servant, as I had mercy on you?' And in anger his master delivered him to the jailers, until he should pay all his debt. So also my heavenly Father will do to every one of you, if you do not forgive your brother from your heart."[31]

It is one thing to say that you should forgive, and another thing to do it. Again, Jesus knows very well that such a forgiving way of life is not natural to our present nature. That is why he makes it such a central part of our daily prayer and life. We need divine help in maintaining such an attitude. Each day we need to pray for forgiveness. Each day we need to remember to forgive. Each day we need to pray to remember to remember.

Remembering that the *who* of another person is more important than the *what* will daily orient us to the right attitude. However, there are some people who just do not seem to appear worth forgiving. I get to know the *who* of them and the *who* is pretty pitiful. Most people really would not like to have gotten to know the *who* of Adolf Hitler, Joseph Stalin, Pol Pot, Mao, Charles Manson, and the like. At least on the surface, these men do not have many redeeming qualities. Likewise, the child abused by a

---

[31] Matthew 18:23-35

religious leader, the victim of incest, and any of us confronted by a pedophile, have little ability—and maybe less desire—to forgive the perpetrator and be in a relationship with them.

Of course, there are a number of reasons to avoid them However, we must struggle with the concept of forgiveness even here. At this point a common misunderstanding about forgiveness stands in our way.

This misunderstanding may be the result of how we frequently respond to an apology. Someone says to us, "I'm sorry", and if we are being nice we say, "That's okay." If forgiveness means negating the offense, then to forgive evil is extremely difficult. A better response than "That's okay," is possibly to say "Yes, what you did hurt me, maybe it was even evil, but if you truly wish to relate to me as a valued human being again, then I will not demand that you receive what you deserve." Hurt and evil are to be acknowledged, the offender if truly sorry is repentant; that is the heart of forgiveness. If someone were to come to their priest and ask for absolution, the heart of the repentance is summed up in a statement such as "I truly intend never to do that again." If they are deceiving themselves and others, and truly do intend to do it again, then they are not seeking to heal a relationship and absolution is not given. Forgiveness is not vengefully withheld from them, it is just not possible to provide; they are not truly seeking reconciliation.

Then there is the situation where the offender never says they are sorry. In such a state, true reconciliation between people may not be possible. However, the victim may still want to move toward the outlook Jesus is promoting but finds it nearly impossible. The block is often because, in a self-protective fashion, we often take on the triple role of judge, jury, and executioner.

Many people unconsciously hold resentments because they find God to be too lax. It is an interesting contradiction. These same people will often view God as being quite harsh with them, but then unconsciously hold resentment, because they find God too forgiving of others. Well-meaning friends and counselors will tell the resentful person that vengeance is the Lord's; put down the triple role and let God take care of the offender. However, secretly, the victim believes that God might forgive the offender without inflicting a righteous measure of pain upon them. So the victim believes that they are the only ones on earth that can make sure the offender pays for their sins.

The major problem with this is not merely putting oneself in God's role, but that there is no power given to be judge, jury, and executioner. In the victim's mind and heart, the offender is guilty and now must pay, but no power is provided by which to make them pay. The victim merely wanders about, carrying the resentment in order to assure the verdict and bring judgment on the offender, but the offender never realizes it. The pain is inflicted in only one direction: toward the victim. This is typically because the victim does not want to pay a further price of violating society's laws and God's commandments in order to carry out the verdict. Vigilantes often do not end well. However, there is a method that is sometimes useful to release the pain. Instead of acting externally on the verdict, begin internally to play through the executioner scenario.

Take dealing with a pedophile as an example. The victim—even the vicarious victim who hears about such horror—must ponder what the perpetrator deserves. Ultimately what they deserve is a slow, painful, death and then being delivered to Hell. Prior to that, think of how that slow, painful death should play out. Maybe first castration? With a dull knife? Now, many a victim may find some initial pleasure in imagining this. But then, realize that you are the executioner: you must be the one to enact this scene. You must personally castrate the person, then slowly kill them, imagining and watching their terror and agony each step of the way. At this point, most people will merely wish for someone else to do horror, not them. But you are the victim, it is to you that the perpetrator

64

"owes" their suffering and pain; pain similar to what the perpetrator inflicted upon the victim.

Now, if you truly can carry through on this, if there is still a glee about inflicting such suffering, you need to further examine your own soul, for you (as is so often the case in a world of oppression and abuse) have now become the oppressor and abuser. You have made another suffer in order to meet your own need. They made you suffer for their perverse sexual need, you have made them suffer for your need to exact revenge. You have merely become the very evil you are meaning to punish. Thankfully, most people will recoil at the thought of inflicting such true horror upon another person. When the dull knife is figuratively offered they choose not to take it. This is forgiveness. The perpetrator owes the victim to suffer reciprocal pain, they owe the victim their life, however the victim chooses not to inflict that pain and take that life: they have said no to the debt, the debt needs not be repaid. The victim has forgiven the offender.

Such forgiveness does not imply that something was okay. In this situation, it does not imply that what the offender did is no longer remembered. It merely means that the *who* is now recognized more than the what. The pedophile is still recognized for who they are; an imperfect human being, one still made in the image of God, but also one who has a severe psychopathology that stills dominates their psyche. I may not castrate them, I may not kill them, but I still will not allow them to be alone with a child. Recognizing the *who* is not some idealized philosophy, it is seeing the person for who they totally are, the good as well as the bad. If they are ever to be healed, it will only be by their own recognition of this as well as that of someone else who totally sees them. This is the healing power of forgiveness, the power that brings each of us into full relationship with God and with each other. In many ways, Hell is defined and populated with those who want neither God nor others. And so they get what they want. Jesus presents the way of heaven: the way of forgiveness, the way of reconciliation, the way of deep, robust relationship.

Temptation and Evil

As we come to the conclusion of Jesus' teaching on prayer, we encounter a most disconcerting and challenging admonition. "Lead us not into temptation, but deliver us from the evil one." I choose to say here "evil one" rather than "evil" because evil has such a generic feel to it. When spoken of generically, evil carries little of the horror that it truly embodies. Hearing of the evil of millions of people killed under Hitler, Stalin, and Mao disturbs us, but our disturbance is nothing compared to viewing a man being beheaded or burned to death, or the picture of aborted baby parts being sold for profit. Evil is always very personal, and so speaking of the evil one brings the fact closer to home.

Pausing and pondering this portion of the Lord's Prayer it is easy to be caught by the oddity of this request. Temptations are considered inducements to immoral actions; seductions to do something forbidden. So why should we need to ask a seemingly good God to not lead us into the very things he is telling us to avoid? Would God actually take us down a path that could potentially lead to our ruin?

The answer is absolutely yes. God does lead people into a time of true testing, one where temptation may be encountered in a most profound manner. It certainly happened to Jesus and he is clearly the pioneer and guide of our spiritual walk. It occurred to him immediately after his baptism in the Jordon. In the Gospel according to Mark, we are told that it was at the very moment after baptism that the Holy Spirit drove Jesus into the wilderness to be tempted by the devil—rather a potent phrase indicating an overwhelming inclination. Mark tells us he was driven, Matthew and Luke rephrase it; for them he was led into the wilderness, and so Jesus tells us to pray, "lead us not…"

If we rightly assume that God is not a cosmic sadist, or merely fickle, then there must be some profound, overarching purpose in being led into the wilderness to confront temptations—

and there is. This purpose is so that each person might be given the opportunity to fulfill their destiny, to become the true being God originally intended them to be. This opportunity will be the dramatic encounter of the ego with the remainder of their being. Our little fish must now confront and cooperate with the remainder of the inhabitants of the ocean of the complete self. It is an encounter that must transpire but is one filled with risk. To face oneself—to strive to become whole, or perfect—may have the ring of an exciting pursuit, but the practical reality is that it is dirty, difficult work.

To do inner spiritual work at first sounds very romantic, but it is also quite dangerous. It is like what transpires for the Hobbits—Frodo, Sam, Merry, and Pippin—in *The Lord of the Rings*. Initially the idea of an adventure appeared so romantic. After the meetings with dangers, wicked creatures, and evil itself, they had to wonder why they embarked on the quest at all. The task of spiritual work and the journey of confrontation with the remainder of the psyche is so dangerous that Jesus urges—even warns—that we pray to God, "lead us not into temptation, but deliver us from the evil one." The danger lies in two places: our own soul and the activity of the devil.

This perilous but necessary task is well demonstrated in Jesus' own experience of temptation and his confrontation with the devil. In the Gospel according to Matthew we hear it like this:

> Then Jesus was led up by the Spirit into the wilderness to be tempted by the devil. And after fasting forty days and forty nights, he was hungry. And the tempter came and said to him, "If you are the Son of God, command these stones to become loaves of bread." But he answered, "It is written, "'Man shall not live by bread alone, but by every word that comes from the mouth of God.'" Then the devil took him to the holy city and set him on the pinnacle of the temple and said to him, "If you are the Son of God, throw yourself down, for it is written, "'He will command his angels

concerning you,'" and "'On their hands they will bear you up, lest you strike your foot against a stone.'" Jesus said to him, "Again it is written, "'You shall not put the Lord your God to the test.'" Again, the devil took him to a very high mountain and showed him all the kingdoms of the world and their glory. And he said to him, "All these I will give you, if you will fall down and worship me." Then Jesus said to him, "Be gone, Satan! For it is written, "'You shall worship the Lord your God and him only shall you serve.'" Then the devil left him, and behold, angels came and were ministering to him.[32]

What is illustrated in this event is what mystics would later refer to as the purgative way. It is the confrontation with the impulses, desires, and demands of the as yet unredeemed soul. This confrontation is otherwise known as the sanctification process, the process of becoming holy. The Eastern Orthodox theologian will call it the work of becoming divine. This is because when a person embarks on the Christian life it begins with a decision and a training of the ego. Even for those baptized as infants, a time of decision must come, a time when the ego decides to take the journey. The ego has made a choice, but there remain within the soul other entities that have not participated in this choice and may even contend against it. These are the powers that lie hidden outside of ordinary consciousness, outside the purview of the ego, things that psychologists have referred to as complexes and archetypes of the unconscious. Though outside ego consciousness, these are still integral parts of the total person, and so must be met, dealt with, finally even befriended.

We see this exemplified in the types of temptations presented to Jesus. He is confronted with the common desires for satisfying physical pleasures, obtaining corporate power over others, and for gaining spiritual power and experiences. On one hand these are generic temptations of the complete person: the body, the soul, and the spirit. We will see later that they are also

---

[32] Matthew 4:1-11

specific encounters of temptations to premature actions specific to Jesus.

The confrontation is necessary for Jesus and for us because these complexes and archetypes which populate our unconscious comprise the wholeness of our personhood; of our complete selves. We must meet them and embrace them if we are to finally live into the likeness of the image of God. However, at the present moment in our lives, these other parts are acting quite independently of our conscious will. It is as if in the ocean of our psyche there is a multitude of other fish swimming quite independently of our little ego-fish—so independently that the ego-fish is unaware of their existence (so we call them unconscious) and many of them are unaware of the ego's existence. The goal in the end is that all of these fish will school together, swimming cooperatively in unison. The task presented the newly baptized ego, the ego that has decided to pursue a life with God, is to now bring these others into that harmony. We once again can see this with our other metaphor of the choir or symphony. The ego is to be the conductor leading the others into a harmony of sound and beauty.

If the ego was as strong as we like to believe it is, and its will as powerful as we imagine, the task of meeting the other parts and bringing them into harmony would not be a problem. Unfortunately, this is not the situation.

These complexes and archetypes within the unconscious ocean of the psyche often carry more power and energy than does the ego and can easily overwhelm it. Merely witness the effects of psychosis and addictions. If that is not worrisome enough, we must realize that it is by means of these inner complexes that the devil gains access and control of our inner lives. It is no wonder that the ego has closed its eyes to the inner world in favor of believing that it is all that exists, for the inner world can be a terrifying place populated with powerful beings, mythic creatures, monsters, and the abode of the devil. We know this because we live with them every night within our dreams. It is no wonder so many people avoid remembering their dreams.

This description of the inner life is exactly how the desert and the wilderness is described in mythology and in the Bible. As such, any civilized man or woman may opt to avoid such a primitive, dangerous, and dirty inner world. However, it is not merely a place of potential horror. It also contains the only road to healing and wholeness. Here is found the road of salvation. It is out of this very place—out of this wilderness of the unconscious inner world—that salvation is to come.

> A voice cries: "In the wilderness prepare the way of the
> LORD; make straight in the desert a highway for our God.
> Every valley shall be lifted up, and every mountain and hill
> be made low; the uneven ground shall become level, and
> the rough places a plain. And the glory of the LORD shall
> be revealed, and all flesh shall see it together, for the mouth
> of the LORD has spoken."[33]

It is in and through the wilderness that God comes to us. It is in the confrontation with the other aspects of the psyche that we become whole and allow ourselves to fully know God. Therefore, the person who has committed themselves to a life with God (this is what was done in baptism) cannot avoid the journey; God will not allow the ego to hide in fear from the destiny of the complete self. Anyone who desires healing, anyone who hopes for a full life, anyone who wishes to know God and to live spiritually will be driven into the wilderness so that life can be found and fulfilled. But it is still a wilderness. Like any true adventurer, we need to go prepared for the journey and the battle.

When we realize that the content of most of our dreams are representations of complexes—the various parts of our psyche, the inhabitants of our inner ocean—then the metaphor of the fish unfolds into a more common experience. The people in our dreams

---

[33] Isaiah 40:3-5

have distinct personalities, separate wills, and desires. Some of them may want things the ego does not want. Some we will enjoy, some will be repulsive. Some we will respect, others we will want to reject. What we find is that all of the desires, thoughts, and emotions contained in these separate parts are, in some manner, integral and vital to our overall life. They were all created by God and therefore all are essentially good. However, when allowed to "swim" independently of the whole, they may be out of balance, and these originally good things may promote harm and even evil.

Take Eros for example, or the desire to unite with another person. Eros is the embodiment of the beauty of love when in the company of respect, and in social conventions such as marriage and true friendship. Eros, when separated from these and taken alone, is lust and even the power of rape. Shakespeare saw it well and in Sonnet 129 relates the degradation of Eros' beauty:

> The expense of spirit in a waste of shame
> Is lust in action; and till action, lust.

All that God created, when brought into harmony with the full self, is beauty incarnate. When separated, it has the potential to become evil incarnate. All things in moderation and in balance is the motto of the way of health and wholeness. Extremes in any manner create a disequilibrium and lead down the path to destruction.

The work of the ego in the wilderness is the labor of bringing harmony to all the disparate parts of the complete self. In the end, all of the "fish" of the psychic "ocean" are to swim in harmony. Today they tend to go each in their own direction and manner. To engender harmony the ego must "befriend" each of the others and gain their allegiance. As it does so, the now God focused ego gains allies in its growth toward the total consciousness of the complete self, the very image of God.

A prerequisite for this work is that the ego has enough strength to deal with each of the unconscious parts. This, however, is not always the case. More often, when the ego comes into contact with an unconscious complex, it is overtaken by the energy of that complex.

For instance, a man who views a scantily clad woman in a beer commercial. The intention of the advertiser was to grab hold of the viewer's attention by sexual innuendo. The advertiser does not try to relate to the desire for a good beverage nor intoxication; neither of those complexes are activated. The advertisement sends messages received by Eros within. How this works is that a "sexual", erotic personality of the inner world gets activated by the image of the woman. If this part has not been brought into harmony with other aspects of the inner world, and if the man has not developed the proper virtuous attitudes, then the "sexual", erotic part's energy will overtake the ego and the ego is then dominated by this energy. It is as if our little fish just got swallowed by a much bigger fish. The man will then stare at the image and, in the shadowy corners of his consciousness, desire to have sex with that woman, and associate the pleasure of this act with the beer. The swallowing of the ego may be seen as a form of psychological possession. The energy of the erotic complex in the unconscious has taken control of the ego and the ego follows along like a slave with a ring in its nose.

The manner in which the ego can be protected from this is either to bring the sexual complex into harmony with other inner aspects that can counterbalance it, or to have sufficiently developed the virtues to combat the possession. Such virtues might be prudence and patience. When the image arises, do not hastily follow the sexual energy that arises, but with patience merely notice it, and then prudence moves the mind onto other matters. It is not the seeing of the image that causes the problem, it is entertaining it that is problematic. Entertaining the image allows the energy in the complex to take hold of the ego. Jesus once taught that "everyone who looks at a woman with lustful intent has already committed adultery with her in his heart."[34] So Jesus indicates that it is not the

---

[34] Matthew 5:29

looking that is the problem, it is the intent. The energy of intent arises from the inner complex which invades and grabs hold of the ego. Grabbing hold of the ego is quite easy for an erotic complex. If ever you thought that the ego and its will power were strong, just place it up against sexuality and addiction. The feebleness of the ego is obvious in such situations.

Likewise, place it up against other complexes such as desire for power, fame, and success, or against striving for spiritual power and experiences. All of these easily overpower the ego. We must realize that willpower is highly overrated.

Frankly, most of the complexes of the unconscious are more powerful than the ego so, again, it is no wonder that the ego wants to isolate itself and believe that it is the only thing in the ocean, an activity we call denial. However, once the ego is compelled to believe it is surrounded by all of the "others" it then wants to believe that it can at least control or get rid of these denizens of the unconscious. This is what we often view as repression. This does not work well in the long run.

For the person seeking wholeness of self and union with God, denial and repression are no longer options. This person must confront the other parts of the complete self so that in the end she or he will be harmonized and whole. Only then can we cry out with the Psalmist; "Bless the Lord, O my soul, and *all* that is within me, bless His holy name." Each must confront the inner personalities we know as complexes, and in doing so run the risk of being possessed by these inner realities. Each must face the "temptation" presented by each of these inner realities and befriend them bringing them into the desired harmony of the interior choir.

If facing the potentially overwhelming power of the inner complex is not bad enough, we then recognize that it is through influencing these unconscious factors that Satan and his demons work to control the ego and so the individual. The inner complex that sees itself as royalty (we all have those imaginations of being a

74

king, a queen, a princess) is constantly being seductively induced to pride by the whispering of the devil into the complex's figurative ear and given a demonic dose of energy. That complex in turn then whispers to the ego that the person deserves power and control over others; constantly nudging the ego to do its bidding until the outer world only sees a person with an authoritarian attitude or worse a despot.

In practical experience, few people ever see or hear the devil. His influence comes through the unconscious. As we earlier saw, God infrequently speaks to the ego, preferring to speak to the whole person, the deep self. In a similar but less integrated fashion, the demonic makes its influence known within the unconscious depths. Then, with the added energy and influence of the demonic, a split-off, independent complex can gain such a tremendous degree of energy that the ego finds itself powerless, and in the sway of that energy. We then witness true demonic oppressions and possessions.

This is the danger and the risk of the spiritual journey, a journey that the lover of God is compelled to take. It is a journey where the ego must confront the powers of the unconscious psyche; powers strong on their own and reinforced by the energy of the demonic. Without the assistance and energy of God, and without the development of the virtues, this endeavor is more than dangerous, it can be spiritually and physically deadly. Witness those who naively take hold of the occult or blindly follow the techniques of the New Age Movement. The unconscious aspects of the psyche are seen to overwhelm their egos and the world observes people with psychoses, in "spiritual crises", and even demonically possessed.

Christians are not immune. Many embark upon the search for spiritual experiences naively and prematurely and run the same risk as the person dabbling in the occult. This is more often encountered in the Pentecostal and Charismatic movements, but in any situation the unprepared ego may be swallowed coming up

75

against the powers in the unconscious and the devil. It is well documented in a book exploring the last days of the Welsh Revival at the end of the 19th century: *War on the Saints*,[35] by Jesse Penn-Lewis. The ego must be prepared through the development of virtues and guidance before seeking spiritual powers and experiences. Premature action is one of the great dangers of encountering the unconscious.

We see this clearly in the temptations of Jesus. There we can see that it is not merely what is being done, but when it is done, that makes an action evil. For Jesus to transform elements, stone into bread or water into wine, is not the issue. It is when. In the end he would transform bread into his body. Becoming king of the nations is not the issue; that will happen, not just yet. To perform a righteous action prematurely is to enact evil. It is not necessarily what we do, but how and when we do it that determines the holiness of it.

Because of the demands of the journey and the dangers to be faced, Jesus teaches a sobering message, pray to God that He not lead you into temptation, and delivers you from the evil one. Pray that the powers of the unconscious psyche will not be too strong for your ego, and that the objective devil is cut off from influencing your unconscious. When that happens—when the ego meets the unconscious accompanied by the divine energy which is the grace of God; when the devil is cut off by the power of God—then these complexes are available to be integrated, and the teamwork of the formerly unconscious complexes and the ego expanded. Then you can move further in the realization of your whole self, and into the knowledge of God.

Much of the spiritual work that has just been described is—in theological language—the *kataphatic* way. It is the manner of practicing the spiritual life utilizing symbols, images, and ideas. There is another path called the *apophatic* way and it is one that

---

[35] Penn-Lewis, Jessie with Evan Roberts (1994). <u>War on the Saints</u>, Thomas Lowe, NY.

avoids images and symbols in favor of a detached, imageless prayer, and an inner emptying.

We began this discussion with the *kataphatic* because it is the way more often chosen by the typical seeker, as it does not demand the extent of ego-denial the *apophatic* way demands; something most people living an average daily life find nearly impossible to accomplish. However, as we read the Lord's Prayer, we are confronted with the possibility that Jesus was recommending this other apophatic way, this way beyond images, beyond a step-by-step confrontation with the contents of the soul leading to a direct plunge into the wilderness encounter of God.

This *apophatic* way is also well trodden, as it is witnessed in the Hesychastic practices of the Christian East, as well as in those of the anonymous English author of the *Cloud of Unknowing* and the Spanish Carmelites in the Christian West. It is also the paradoxical way presented by the great German mystic, Meister Eckhart as well as a spirituality which metaphorically mirrors much of the early metaphysical understanding of life-after-death. It is with an understanding of life-after-death that we can conceive of the apophatic metaphor of a direct plunge toward God through the purifying and sanctifying wilderness.

How do we understand the afterlife? Up to relatively recently most of the Christian world conceived of bodily death as a moment of transition into a continuing existence of purification and increasing union with God. Throughout history and across various cultures there has been the common conception that upon the death of the body the soul would enter a land of the dead, whether that be Hades, Sheol, a Bardo state, Valhalla, or any number of various other notions. One of the great changes that occurred with the resurrection of Jesus was that now a new possibility was established. The soul no longer needs go to the land of the dead but could enter one of the heavens.

Equally, across history and cultures there has been a common conception about heaven. It was the land of the gods. In some places we find nine heavens, in other places seven, in still others an even greater multitude but to simplify the matters, we will stick with the common Biblical conception of three heavens[36]: the earthly paradise, the celestial paradise, and the Empyrean, or the Heaven of Heavens. It was to this Heaven of Heavens—the third heaven—that St. Paul journeyed at one time. The transit from the moment of bodily death to full life with God in the Heavens of Heavens was one of continued growth and purification. This concept would be later modified by the Roman Catholic Church into a dogma of Purgatory. Staying with the earlier conception, most Christians believed that if they had not completed their purification toward union with God while in the body they would continue to do so in the afterlife; a time of dealing with the temptations not overcome during the bodily life.

The notion is that if you have not prevailed over the desires for the pleasures of the world, but are a member of the Body of Jesus Christ, then after the death of your physical body you join Jesus in the earthly paradise and there deal with these desires. Likewise, with more subtle desires you may join Jesus to deal with these in the celestial paradise. Only those who had sustained a deep, abiding relationship with Jesus in while in their physical bodies go directly to the Heaven of Heavens. This is a simple explanation of what makes a "Saint". Whereas all Christians are considered "holy ones", or saints in some manner (only saints go to heaven), those persons who came to know themselves and know God most closely are the ones who would be transported to the Heaven of Heavens after death, bypassing the purification process of the intermediary heavens.

A wonderful story surrounding the life of St. Cuthbert of Lindisfarne illustrates this belief. The story is that one night, while still a boy, the young Cuthbert was in the fields of Northumbria

---

[36] Refer to the Genesis story where out of the uncreated Heaven of Heavens are formed two created heavens.

watching over the sheep. In many ways it was a typical night, with the stars blinking brilliantly in the dark sky. While watching that clear sky Cuthbert's vision was captivated by a bright beam of light flowing out of the depth of heaven and proceeding down toward earth coming to rest east of him. As he fascinatedly watched, he saw within the light angels traveling to earth. Soon after they reversed course and returned up the light, but this time there was an even brighter light in their midst as they disappeared back into the depths of heaven. Not long after, Cuthbert learned that on that very night holy Aidan of Lindisfarne had died. Cuthbert then knew that he had witnessed the soul of St. Aidan being carried to the Heaven of Heavens by the angels.

The metaphysical concept of Purgatory is a dogma required to be believed by Roman Catholics. However, the metaphorical construct of the transit of the heavens is useful for all of us as a description of the spiritual life that Jesus may be presenting in the Lord's Prayer.

The typical spiritual life is a journey through the soul, much like the journey through the heavens. We confront the passions, the desires, and the impulses of a self-dominated life and learn to overcome their dominion and integrate them into the wholeness of life. This is accomplished in what mystical literature calls the Purgative Way and what St. John of Cross referred to as the Dark Night of the Soul. The soul is then confronted by and must deal with processes and energies deeper within, something called the Illuminative Way, or the Dark Night of the Spirit. Only after this is the Unitive Way attained. When Jesus proposes that we ask the Father to "lead us not into temptation" he may be indicating that—if we will—we can take a more direct path to the depths of heaven and the depths of union with God. This is a more direct path than the *kataphatic*, but one demanding full renunciation and emptying of the ego so to fly directly to an identity with the deep self.

Cyprian Smith, a monk of Ampleforth Abbey in Yorkshire, summarized this in a precise and articulate manner in his book about Meister Eckhart.[37]

> There are two quite different paths to our spiritual goal…[i]f, as many have done, we compare the spiritual journey to the ascent of a mountain, the two paths appear in this way: the first is a winding path, approaching the summit gradually, pausing at each stage. It is slow, but thorough. The second assaults the summit directly, ascending the steep rock-face without hesitation or delay. The descent afterwards may be slow and gradual, but the initial ascent is not. It is a dangerous path, but it attains its goal and is right for those who are suited to it.

> This first path is that of much modern psychoanalysis, perhaps especially of the Freudian and Jungian type. The penetration of the deeper levels of the mind, the filtering through into consciousness of the contents of the unconscious mind, is slow and gradual. As the unconscious reveals itself through dreams and symbols, and through impulses never experienced previously, none of the "revelations" are dismissed or discarded. They are pondered over, accepted and worked through gradually, though without letting ourselves be trapped or overwhelmed by them. If we patiently and persistently follow this serpentine path into the depths of ourselves, we shall discover, as the cost of some danger, unsuspected sources of energy for good or for ill…and if we follow the path right to the end, beyond the merely psychological, we shall finally come to the deepest level of all, the "treasure hidden in the field" of which the gospel speaks—the pure, undifferentiated consciousness, stripped of all that is egotistical and personal, the central core of our nature, where the light of God shines.

---

[37] Smith, Cyprian (1987). The Way of Paradox. Darton, Longman, Todd. London. pgs. 11-13.

This is a great path, but it is not the path of Eckhart…His approach…aims straight for the goal, the deepest layer of the mind, the pure essence of consciousness which is the Image of God in us. If, as we penetrate further towards the centre, images and symbols arise, promises of new desires and new possibilities, they are to be ignored and passed by, until the Central Core is reached, where we can become rooted and grounded in God. Then, strengthened and enlightened by that, we ascend slowly to the light, unlocking caverns and treasures on our way, if that seems right. But the first prerequisite is to find God in the deepest core of ourselves, and this is done by detachment, by letting go of all in us that is not God, until a spark of awareness awakens in us, which Eckhart calls "the Birth of God in the soul".

Returning to our metaphor of the fish and ocean, the first way is for the ego/fish to get to know the other fish in the ocean and then coming together as a harmonious, whole inner life handing itself to God. The second way is for the ego/fish to renounce and give no energy to anything that is not God. The fish rejects its own desires and impulses as well as those it confronts as it focuses a piercing attention on God, an attention that is still focused within through the deep self beyond the parts to the whole.

Both ways present dangers. The first is that the other contents of the unconscious will overwhelm the ego and so possess it, and the second is that the ego can delude itself to thinking that it is rejecting the inner images when it is actually merely temporarily repressing them, an act that almost assures the ego of being controlled by an inner complex.

The danger of the second, direct way is to confuse repression and denial for detachment. Detachment is to recognize a thought, impulse, complex, and then give it no energy, to shift attention back to the obscurity of God. Repression and denial is to have the attitude that such thoughts and impulses are not, and should not, even be present. Detachment recognizes their presence and consciously and willingly shifts away. Repression and denial do not "see" the problem. It would be like reading a good book. A sharp sound may momentarily distract you but, after noticing the origin of the sound, you turn your attention back to your book. That is renunciation and detachment. Repression is when you are reading that same book and a sound occurs and you are either so absorbed in the book or you have put on ear muffs so that you do not even hear it. But if the sound was of an out-of-control car coming straight at you it is better to have heard it and moved, only then getting back to your reading.

As is noted, both paths hold their dangers. However, it appears that Jesus may be promoting the second path over the first. The gospels tell us that the Holy Spirit took Jesus out into the desert to encounter much of what appears to be the first path, a path many of us now take primarily because we are not ready for the extent of detachment and renunciation demanded on the second path. Since the gospels are clear that Jesus was led into the wilderness to be tempted by Satan, and Jesus subsequently teaches us to pray against just that, it makes one wonder if he was not advocating the *apophatic* path, a path first intently seeking the face of God and then subsequently confronting the energies within the soul. As Cyprian Smith described it to "become rooted and grounded in God. Then, strengthened and enlightened by that, we ascend slowly to the light, unlocking caverns and treasures [dealing with the rest of the psyche] on our way".

Jesus had to walk the path that confronts all that pulls us away from God, a path that took him into a face-to-face confrontation with the Devil. Jesus knows the difficulty of such a confrontation and warns us to pray that this might be avoided. But, as with so many prayers, we often do not want all that an answered prayer may bring. To be delivered from the path that Jesus walked in the wilderness, to go the apophatic way, entails a deep level of renunciation and detachment. So far, practical experience tells us that most people do not desire that degree of self-emptying and so end up taking the kataphatic fork in the road that leads through the desert and a confrontation with the Devil. Either way, Jesus knows that as we enter the intimate embrace of the Father we walk a path of peril, a path where God's grace is direly needed, a grace which arises in response to our prayer "lead us not into temptation, but deliver us from the evil one."

The Essence of Jesus' Prayer

We have now touched at least some of the essence of Jesus' prayer. We have begun to grasp an idea of God's purpose and desire for us and the manner by which we can find the fullness of love, union, and friendship with our Creator; our Father, our God. It begins when we truly and completely face ourselves.

To face ourselves we first need to know that God is intimately involved with us and loves us as a Father desiring only the best for us. We need to submit ourselves to the truth that he is our completion and so surrender to his ways and desires; to realize that God knows our basic needs and will meet them; not only our basic needs, but the depths of our spiritual hungers, hungers that He satisfies with Himself, the heavenly manna.

Having this knowledge and experience in place, God then places before us the task of life: to become the complete, full people that he has imagined and destined us to be, bringing our full person into a deep, intimate relationship with Himself. A relationship that is fulfilled in the enlightening of the complete person, for as both St. Antony of the Desert, and St. Catherine of Sienna have said: to know God, to love God fully, one must know oneself.

This journey of self-knowledge takes a difficult and dangerous road, one that demands self-exploration and introspection. It involves the difficulty of forgiving others; the task of realizing that often our resentments are merely the projections of our own unconscious onto another person. It demands recognizing and halting the tendency to remove splinters from other people's eyes, a ploy we use to distract ourselves from seeing the beams lodged in our own eyes. It means facing the hatreds, the resentments, the revulsions we have toward others, and then forgiving others. Only by coming to forgive others will we truly be able to face and embrace our own inner complexes; an embrace that must occur if we are to bring all of ourself to God. An embrace that must occur if we are to be whole, completed, and perfect in the end. This desire for wholeness is a yearning God has placed within each of us as our destiny. A longing articulated by Jesus when we said, "You therefore must be perfect, as your heavenly Father is perfect."[38] This is an embrace that allows us to be the images of God in which we were created.

This is all the grand task of life, a task summarized into a few short lines spoken by Jesus. Contained in such a concise package is the fullness of spiritual life. The Lord's Prayer is no longer seen as a mere technique or formal prayer; no longer a rehearsed chant; but it is the paradigm for our spiritual life. Each time we recite it, we no longer experience it just as a manner of talking to God during a period of "prayer", but as a daily reminder of how to make the whole of our existence a living conversation with God. Each time we recite the Lord's Prayer we indicate to our souls the path that leads to our destiny. In every moment that we say it we pick up our cross—our destiny—and walk into the light that God has imagined for each of us, the light of being a person fully awake, fully alive, fully the image and now likeness of God.

---

[38] Matthew 5:48

www.ingramcontent.com/pod-product-compliance
Lightning Source LLC
LaVergne TN
LVHW091206080426
835509LV00006B/857